GRACE CAME

in the

MOURNING

A Widow's Awakening

Trish Stanbery

ISBN 979-8-88751-263-1 (paperback)
ISBN 979-8-88751-264-8 (digital)

Christian Faith Publishing
832 Park Avenue
Meadville, PA 16335
www.christianfaithpublishing.com

Printed in the United States of America

CONTENTS

PREFACE

Grace Came in the Mourning was created by the call of the Lord. This book is the first book that I have ever written. I pray that its acceptance from the readers will be as God intended.

I want this book to show the emphasis on God and the grace He bestowed on my life in what was my very darkest hour. This book will illustrate pieces of my life story, but the importance of this story is not that you learn about me but the true Author at hand, Jesus Christ. In this book, you will meet an innocent young girl raised within a Christian home her entire life, a girl who was so blind by deception, *but* then there was Jesus when her world suddenly came to a stop.

As the reader of this book, I encourage you to please take in each word, open your heart and your mind to the truths that will be shared, and listen for that still, small voice of the Lord. Sharing my story will not come without many tears as I begin to write this book. I have tried to run from the idea of writing this book for months now, but that call keeps coming back full circle. God has a purpose and a plan for His story with me to be shared, perhaps to touch the life of another soul He is calling to him.

This book will be unlike most books concerning grief. This book will not only later go on to cover my healing and my journey through the grief of the loss of my late husband but will be meant to illustrate the movement of God in my life and His drawing me to Him. It is my prayer that this book will be written not in my own words but in the words that God instills within me to share.

ACKNOWLEDGMENTS

I would like to dedicate this book first and foremost to my Lord and Savior Jesus Christ as well as to my wonderful husband Jacob Stanbery, to my two sweet children Riley and Emma Mulgrew, who have walked this journey with me, to my parents Eddie and Debbie, my siblings Jennifer and Perry, who allowed me to lean on them when I was broken. To my sister-in-law Lauren for being the vessel used by God in my healing. Everyone has played a part in God's divine plan to draw me closer to Him.

I also want to not only dedicate this book to my late husband, Robert Matthew Wall. I hope to honor his legacy as he played the biggest role in God's awakening in my Life.

May the Lord use the stories that He created within our lives—of bringing us all together for His glory—to touch the lives of others who may not know Him as their personal Lord and Savior.

CHAPTER 1

From the Beginning

I want to take you back a few years and introduce you to a young girl named Trish Bodford. If you do not know already, that young girl was me. I grew up in a small rural town of Mocksville, North Carolina. I was raised in a highly conservative Christian home along with two other siblings. My baby brother Perry and my elder sister Jennifer. We were blessed to have two wonderful Christian parents, Eddie and Debbie Bodford. Our parents were both saved in their young adult lives. My mother is the one who had the privilege to lead my dad to Christ when they were just beginning to date. My dad, not much longer, felt the calling of God on his life to be a preacher, and he answered that call. They were always faithful to church and the work of Christ.

As soon as I came into the world, my parents had me in church. I have very vague memories of my first church home at Liberty Baptist, where my dad accepted the call to preach. By the time I was one year old, my parents felt the call to move their membership to another church. Sometime between the ages of one and two, I was then introduced to my new church, Trinity Baptist. Trinity would then become the church in that my entire life would become so heavily involved till I reached the age of twenty-five.

From grades K5 to twelfth grade, I attended a Christian school. My parents worked so hard to be able to make sure their children were able to attain a strong biblically sound education. I was surrounded by the teaching of the Bible every day of the week. I was in church every time the doors were open.

When I became of the age of fifteen, I began to sing in the church choir. Every Saturday, with my parents, I visited my dad's bus route down in Southmont-Lexington. We would go out and visit children and their parents who didn't have a way to church, and my dad drove a bus provided by the church to be able to pick these people up and bring them to the services and take them home.

I later became a Sunday school teacher for toddlers when I reached the age of seventeen. After I graduated from the Christian school, I went off to a very well-known Bible college. Some would say that to look at me, I had it all. I was a young *Christian* girl with the world at my feet to live for the Lord. I remember a time, just like it was yesterday, that at the very young age of five years old, I was taken by the hand, and I was led outside of the older church building, where I then knelt at the bottom two steps with our church song leader's wife, Mrs. Crystal Hilton. She opened her Bible and began to explain the death of Christ to me and what it meant for me. I then bowed my head and repeated the prayer that she instructed me to repeat after her if I wanted to go to heaven when I died. I did. I repeated that prayer. I was now *saved!*

I later followed that up with baptism at a much older age. I went through the rest of my life believing I was saved. I was good. I never questioned it. I just kept living the life I was taught to live. Later down the road, the unthinkable happened. I found myself within a relationship I shouldn't have been in, and I was greatly mistreated in a way that I will not go into. That was the beginning of the downward spiral of my oh-so-great life.

I later found myself in yet another relationship that I shouldn't have been in, but I rebelled against my parents' advice because I loved him and knew what was best for me. That relationship didn't last, but I received two very sweet, wonderful children from that relationship. I believe today that God has a plan for both of their lives. After that relationship ended, I spiraled even more out of control. I became bitter. I became angry at God, and I took myself out of church completely. I decided from now on, I was taking care of myself. From that moment, I felt no one cared about me or my struggles, and I needed to look out for myself.

I lived a life sleeping around and drinking alcohol every time I walked out my doors. I surrounded myself with new friends who would drink with me and have a good time. I was finally happy for the most part. Yeah, I know I just said I was happy. If you have grown up in a Christian atmosphere at all and are saved, you would probably tell me, "But, Trish, how could you be saved and be happy living a

3

life that God clearly stated that he disapproved of?" Well, that's just it: I wasn't saved. If you recall back to the preface of this book, I stated that you would learn about a young girl who was so blind by deception. Well, that girl was me. This is where you learn of the massive hold of deception that Satan had over my life.

I found myself living my life the way I wanted. I was happy. I had freedom, or so I thought. I went to parties; I went on numerous dates, with some of them resulting in nothing more than mere *hookups*. In other words, I placed myself in situations where most would call me a slut. Boy, I did nothing for my *Christian* reputation.

I also hurt the ones who loved me the most, my parents. You see I adopted an I-don't-care attitude. I was the middle child, as you have already learned, and anyone reading here who is a middle child knows that we can be overlooked at times, or at least that is how we feel, always left to ourselves and cheering ourselves on in our endeavors.

Well, that is an emotion that Satan began to prey on and used against me. I always felt alone in my life. I always felt that whether good or bad, my parents never really seemed to care about what I was feeling or going through in life. It always seemed that their focus was on their son or elder daughter. Satan used this to turn me to others for advice and guidance in my life that kept me inching away from my family a little at a time.

There were so many times that I would get upset and hurt by my family that I felt, *Why do I even care? Just create a new family.* However, I have always been close to my sister, and she and I have always been not only sisters by blood but have been best friends. Jen and I have always been there for each other through some of our life's struggles. Anyone who knows us will tell you that when we are together, we have a good time, always laughing and cracking jokes or playing pranks on each other or other people. I believe this relationship is what kept me from ever truly walking away and cutting ties with my family, and for that, I am so thankful.

Though my sister and I had a strong bond, I still pulled away often. I would see something or hear something within my family walls that would later echo in my mind as to why my family didn't care about me. So like in days past, I turned to my friend Jack Daniels. I started to notice that my alcohol intake was gradually increasing. I was a very strong whiskey or bourbon drinker, and I found that my tolerance was increasing greatly. I could drink more and more and barely feel it. So I would drink even more to get that high that alcohol brings.

I was a happy drunk, if there ever was one. I laughed and laughed till I would pass out. This became almost a daily occurrence. Because, well, who doesn't love to laugh? I was stern about the fact that I would never drink around my children or allow them to see me drink. Because of that rule, I felt that I was okay. I told myself that I didn't have a problem.

Well, even all the liquor couldn't hide the fact of the pit feeling of loneliness. I felt happy, I had a great career, and I loved my work. I had two great kids; I had a bunch of crazy fun friends. I loved my life, except that I always felt alone. I didn't have a healthy love life, so I felt that must be the reason I feel so alone, so then I made it a quest to find Mr. Right.

I later signed on to that awful, repulsive dating app called Tinder. I swiped on that thing daily, almost to the point I was kind of obsessed with it. It then became more like a daily game to see whom I could get interested in me. Wow. Looking back, what a dangerous trap that was.

I then became brave and started meeting these fellows I knew nothing about. I would go with the intention that this is just a date, or as my friends called it, it was a free meal. Though I never went with that intention to be bought a meal and go, I was looking to fulfill a void I couldn't shake. Little did I know it was just another trap of the devil to ruin me.

See, even though I thought I was saved, I wasn't, and the protection of God wasn't on me. I was open prey to Satan and his devices. He would send some of the best-looking men—who I felt I was never in their league—my way. And these men flirted; they charmed me. They gave me the attention that I felt I needed and wanted in life. All they did was talk enough charm till they got what they wanted from me, then they were gone—well, until they were feeling dry and no one else was taking their bait. I was stupid, and I fell for it more often than I should have. What's worse is the deception of the daily lie that Satan kept telling me, that I was having fun, and I was happy. I was just a drunk looking for attention.

I found myself in a place that scared me. My eyes began to open a little bit. One morning, I found myself dazed and confused from the night prior. I couldn't remember much of that night. I just knew I had had a lot to drink and that I spent time with a guy whom I was starting to see frequently, someone I liked and trusted.

This guy had a reputable business that he owned. He was a father, and he was very easy on the eyes. He always was so happy to see me and treated me like I was the one of interest. That night, I had gone to his place to meet him after work. He had called and asked if I wanted to hang out and go swimming. I was delighted to say yes. I arrived to find some of his workhands there as well, I stood around chatting, waiting for them to leave so I could spend some time alone with my date. Well, they never seemed like they were leaving any time soon, and my date kept encouraging me to go change into my swimsuit and join him in the pool, that he had picked up my favorite ales to drink, so I did just that. I went and changed then met him out back at the pool and slowly took my time emerging into what seemed like icy waters.

Once I was comfortable swimming around, he decided to come over and float around with me. That is when the drinks began to be handed to me one after another. His workhands finally left, but not long after they were gone, we were greeted by a couple of his male friends, who decided to join us.

By this time, I had already drunk six bottles of ale, and I was only beginning to feel slightly buzzed. Well, he kept joking that I haven't had enough until I was truly giddy, so he kept pumping them into me. After that, my memories faded. I can only recall pieces of what happened to me that night. I dropped my walls with a man I trusted, and

I shouldn't have. I can't prove anything, but I feel I was drugged that night and taken advantage of by all the men there.

That next morning, I struggled to remember anything. I don't even remember how I got home. Later that day, bits and pieces started to emerge in my mind, and I found myself crying and ashamed that I had allowed myself to get so out of control that I didn't see what was coming myself. That day, I decided to dial way back on my drinking, and I paused my Tinder account for a long time.

I had a membership to another dating website that I had forgotten I had. I never visited it much because it seemed lame, and there was never any interaction. One night, I had a notification in my e-mail that I had received a message on this site from someone. I went through the steps to recover my sign-in information. Considering that I had forgotten I was on the site, I couldn't recall my password to get back in.

I finally got in and read the message. As I was reading the polite greeting from a local Rowan County boy, he was online and direct messaged me a quick little, "Hello, you're online!" followed by a little smiley face. We ended up chatting for a little bit of time, mostly about how lame the site was. He was getting ready to delete his account when my profile popped up, so he decided to check it out. This intriguing guy and I ended up chatting online every night for three solid months before he ever got the nerve to ask me on our first date.

This is where things started to seem a little more hopeful in my life again, and this time, I was going to be wiser on how I conducted myself, and my guard was up. I couldn't allow myself to be found dazed and confused again and wondering if I had just been raped? I learned my lesson. Dating online was dangerous, and you couldn't trust anyone. I find it a little laughable really because I continued to date online. I am thankful that I never was found dead in a ditch somewhere.

I did approach dating online in a more responsible way. I made sure going forward that someone knew about this date, always knew of my location, and would check in at the end of the date to make sure I was safe and home okay.

This intriguing man whom I have chatted with for three months picked me up on his motorcycle, and we enjoyed a nice, scenic ride through the country back roads. We stopped for a bottle of water at the local coffee shop and sat outside and enjoyed a respectful conversation. This man was Robert Wall. We went on three more dates, and we both felt the pursuance to chase a relationship together was just simply not there for either of us. However, this man ended up becoming one of my closest and dearest friends. I would later go on to continue my search for Mr. Right.

CHAPTER 2

Trying to Fill the Void of Loneliness

After things were decided between Robert and me that we would probably be better off as friends, I started to feel that void a little deeper. That's just great; more friends are just what I need in my life. I was starting to feel my friends list grow, but that lonely feeling kept growing even more. By this time, I was truly trying to figure out what it was that was causing this void I couldn't seem to shake. I kept coming back to the fact it had to be that I didn't have a man in my life. I started to feel broken, unworthy, and not good enough. Why was it that I couldn't seem to find a good man who loved the Lord?

As I asked myself this question. I thought, *Well, Trish, you have turned your back on all that you were raised on. You have turned your back on God.* I remembered a story my mom shared with me about her desire to have a godly man in her life. She wanted it so much that she fasted for seven days, asking God to send her the man he had for her, one who would love her, be faithful to her, and would love Him and serve Him with her. As I sat on my floor pondering her story, I decided, well if it worked for her, it would work for me.

That day, I decided I was going to fast and pray. I had confessed to God my sinful ways and apologized for the way that I chose to live my life, and I asked for forgiveness. I told Him that I was tired of habitual dating if you could even call it dating, that I just wanted to meet a man who was saved and loved Him, a man who would guide me and lead me in serving Him. You see, at this point in my life, I had enough knowledge to know something was missing for me. However, I didn't realize it was the Lord. I still believed I was saved simply because I repeated the Sinner's prayer at the age of five. I felt that if I went back to my roots, things would start to improve for me, and if I made God a priority like I had been taught, He would send me the man who was missing in my life.

After a week of my fasting and praying, I decided to hang up my Tinder account and trust that God would miraculously bring this man into my life. I logged back into my Tinder account to properly delete the entire thing. When I logged in, I quickly got distracted by the numerous messages that I had from men who had matched up with me. As I casually read through some of them, a brand-new message pinged me. I decided to view this man's profile, and I was intrigued by it, so I responded.

The conversation started with witty little remarks to one another to the point we both realized we approved of each other's personalities. The conversation began to grow deeper, and about after an hour into our texting each other back and forth on this app, he asked me if I knew Christ as my Lord and Savior. You could pick my jaw up off the floor. I was flabbergasted. Did he just ask me if I was saved? What? Could this be?

I needed more information to know for sure. I told him how I was raised and that, yes, I received Christ as my Savior when I was five years old. I told him that my dad was the deacon of the church that I had grown up in, that my dad was also a preacher. We began to discuss our favorite preachers, and it just so happened to be that C. T. Townsend was holding the huge tent revival meeting in Burlington, North Carolina, that just wouldn't shut down. God had seemed to be all over that revival, and souls were being saved left and right.

That night, he told me that his mom had just attended it and that he wanted to go. Then out of nowhere, he blurted out, "I think meeting you tonight wasn't by accident. I think you and I should go there together before this thing ends."

I sat there reading and rereading his last message, trying to catch my breath. *Is this happening to me right now? I know I just fasted and prayed for this, but this was a faster response from God than I thought I would receive.*

I sat there in disbelief, but without further hesitation, I told him I agree and accept his invitation to go to this revival. He picked me up that very next evening. For safety measures, I asked him to pick me up at my parent's home. I figured if this man was a pawn, he would flee at the thought of meeting my parents for our very first time meeting each other. He didn't flinch. He was happy to do so.

That night he greeted me in a nice suit and tie and five red roses. On our ride to the revival, he asked me if I knew why he chose exactly five red roses. I politely responded with a head nod of no. He looked at me and smiled and said, "Five is the number of grace." I feel we were meant to meet, and this was a notion of God's grace. That has never left me.

The revival was a little over an hour away, so we had plenty of windshield time to chat and get to know each other a little bit more. He shared his personal story with me about his life story of being in the military and coming back home with severe PTSD and his road to salvation, and though I would love to share his powerful testimony, it isn't mine to share. I will share a part that began the tugging process within my spirit beginning to be drawn to the Lord. He shared with me that during his darkest hour that night, he searched the web for anything to help him overcome what he was battling, and he stumbled onto some old-fashioned preaching. The sermon he stumbled on was a sermon on hell and making sure that you are saved. That night alone in the dark in his apartment he received Christ as his Savior.

Listening to him, I began to feel a presence in that car. I got choked up, and I felt a little knock on my heart's door. I believe this was the moment God began to draw me to him. I still did not comprehend what I felt, but I know it was powerful.

As we arrived at the revival meeting, it had just begun, and they were up singing. The minute we stepped on the grounds to that tent, that powerful presence I had felt in the car just amplified. Brother C. T. Townsend preached on your last chance. He preached on hell. He preached on not wasting your last chance to get things right with the Lord and get saved. He preached on God's eventually passing you over to a reprobate mind. God will only call you for so long before He says, "You have denied Me for the last time." That night, I felt something tug at me, but I told myself it was emotional thinking. I was saved. I said the prayer. God heard my prayer and sent this man to me.

He and I dated for a while. Unfortunately, we lived in sin. We didn't live together, but we may as well have. We were already living as if were married. Even in this relationship, I kept seeking out God. I began to do Bible devotions with this new love interest. I was blissfully happy.

But then something began to happen. The more we started to read our Bibles and pray together, the more he began to get convicted about how our relationship was. He began to discuss his feeling with me about it and how he felt God was convicting him over our sleeping together. But it kept getting pushed away till one day he broke up with me. He told me that he couldn't continue like this unless we were married, and he wasn't ready for that commitment yet. I got angry and begged him not to. I loved him. I asked him why we couldn't just keep dating and growing and leave sleeping together off the table. He agreed to that, but unfortunately, our chemistry and lustful nature were too powerful for us. After already taking it there, it was hard to stop.

As it continued, he continued to feel the heat. He called me up and told me he just simply couldn't do this. This breakup lasted a week and we were right back where we started. It continued for another month. I remember praying for this man every single day and blindingly asking God to bless this relationship. I felt and just knew in my heart that he was the one. But come on, Trish. God will never bless a relationship that's living in sin.

After another month of this roller-coaster ride, he ended it for the third time. I struggled. I didn't eat, I didn't sleep, and I barely functioned for weeks. I questioned God every day, "Why did You give this man to me and then take him away?" I couldn't see then what I see now. Later down the road, I would learn the purpose of this man wasn't necessarily to be a love interest. He was used by God for a season.

Remember how I told you about my going back to my roots, my fasting, my asking for forgiveness? I believe in this very moment in my heart of hearts, God took notice of my prayer and my fast. When you fast and pray, God looks at the heart, and your answer may not always be subject to the thing you're praying for. I believe God heard my prayer and saw my need to be rescued and saved. He was beginning to shake me. However, I was continuing to be deceived by the lie that I was saved because I repeated the Sinner's prayer. God saw that my relationship with this man was going backward, and He ended it. At the time, I didn't see or understand this.

I thought of this man daily, and I still prayed for him for weeks. I remember getting so mad after a phone call with him, my mother had called me just minutes after I hung up on him. After I responded to her call, she asked me if I was okay because she could hear in my voice that something seemed wrong. I began to vent to her about how frustrated I was with this man, that I loved him, and I felt God brought him to me, so I don't understand why this was happening.

She began to give me some hard love and hard spiritual truth. She made the statement to me: "Tricia, honey, you both were living a life that God couldn't bless. You were sleeping together as though God would somehow overlook it. I just can't see how you cannot be convicted over this."

I remember getting frustrated, and I spoke back with pride: "Mom, I have never felt convicted over how I chose to live my life."

She, without hesitation, responded, "Oh, Tricia, that worries me for you."

That moment washed off my back like pure water, I never thought of it again. My mind and heart could not let go of this man. I called up my best guy friend Robert Wall. I went to his apartment for some guy advice on how I could fix this with this man. After listening to me cry and pour my heart out about how much I loved him and couldn't understand why he keeps breaking up with me and then comes back, Robert's advice was to leave him alone. I felt it was playing on my emotions, and it was hard. I felt this man loved me and that was why he couldn't stay away longer than a week.

Robert was frustrated with me; he was frustrated with this man I couldn't let go of. He told me that I needed to ignore this guy, that I deserved way better than that. He refused and forbade me to answer his calls or see him again. I told Robert that I would try to do better and just let him go, but it was difficult for me.

At this time, Robert made the choice that he couldn't trust me to do this, so he thought it wise that he should spend more time with me so I wouldn't go back to this man out of loneliness. This worked for the time being. But in my heart, I was struggling. Robert had plans to go to the beach that week with some friends. He had been there most of the week and would be returning home in a few days.

He called me one evening to check on me to see how I was getting along. I told him that I had just received a text message from this man, telling me that he missed me and wanted to take me to dinner. I was sitting in my car at the gas station, contemplating saying yes and going to meet him.

Robert wasn't having it. He told me that I better not even respond and to take my butt back home. I told him it was a struggle because my heart longed to see him. Robert responded, "Get over yourself and go home."

After whining about it, I finally told him okay, and I did just that. Within five minutes of arriving home, my phone rang, and it was Robert once again, checking to make sure I did as I promised I would. He then reported to me that he was loading his stuff in his truck and was heading back home, that he shouldn't have left me. He was home within four and a half hours. He kept me very busy for the weeks to come.

CHAPTER 3

Is This the Answer to Filling the Void?

As the weeks passed, my friendship with Robert began to blossom. The thought of this other man began to fade. Robert called me practically daily, and we would chat for an hour or two, going on about our day, and then before you know it, the phone call would turn into, "I'm hungry. Let's go grab a bite to eat," so we would meet up for supper and then would retire back at his place to catch whatever college football game that would be playing. Most of the time, it was our beloved Clemson Tigers.

In all honesty, I never watched sports that much unless it was baseball, I am a Braves girl. However, Robert got me into watching the games with him. A typical night for us when I didn't have my children would be ordering takeout from Romano's of our favorite dish of baked ziti. We would find our comfy spots on his couch with food in hand and sit, and as I watched the game, he would yell at the screen from play to play. Then he would always pass out before the game would end, and I would have to write the ending scores for him to find when he woke up. Most times, it was on a sticky note stuck to his forehead. I would then clean up our mess, toss a blanket on him, and lock up and head for home.

My brother and his fiancée had an engagement/bridal shower cookout a few weeks later. This event had been planned for some time, and I had forgotten about it, considering I was just trying to hold my head up after a difficult breakup. Lauren had called to remind me of this event. After I spoke to her, I got highly emotional and cried like a baby. I would like to say they were tears of joy that my baby brother finally found a girl who was able to nail his feet to the floor and make him want to settle down, but that was not the case. My tears were because I was supposed to have had a plus-one with me to this event, but he broke up with me.

Robert just happened to call me during this crying charade that I was having for myself and immediately knew I was crying and asked me what was wrong. I told him there was nothing wrong. I would be fine and didn't want to talk about it. Deep down, I was a little bitter at him for keeping me away from the man I loved.

The next day, I was to meet Robert at his apartment after work. He played baseball with a group from the company that he worked for, and he asked me if I would go with him to his games and practices when I could, so I went with him to his first practice that season. In the truck on the ride there, he brought up the crying. He told me he was smart enough to know I was lying when I said I was fine and wanted to know what was going on with me. I told him the truth. I told him it upset me that he kept me from seeing this man, though I understood why, that my soon-to-be sister-in-law called last night to remind me of this event I am to be at, that I had planned to go with this man as my date. Now I must go alone, and I dreaded it. Robert could tell immediately how much this bothered me, and without a skip in time, he said, "You're not going alone. I am going with you."

I was surprised by this jester but happily accepted his offer.

He did as he said, and he accompanied me to this event. Unfortunately, we showed up in Robert's time zone, so we were fashionably late. As we parked the truck and got out, we started to make our way to where everyone was. It seemed like all eyes were on us. I could just hear the whispers as we approached them all. "Who is that with Trish?"

Lauren immediately approached me the minute I was away from Robert and asked me who he was. I simply told her, "That is my best friend. He felt bad about me having to come alone since you-know-who and I are no longer together."

She elbowed me and, in her very direct voice, stated, "Well, I don't know about this other dude, but why are you two not dating? Obviously, there is chemistry between the two of you."

I simply laughed at her and said, "Yeah, right. He is nothing more than my bestie."

As the night went on, my dad watched Robert closely. He watched him watch over me even from a distance, something I didn't pick up on at the time. My dad asked me who he was, seeing how my family had never met Robert before now. I told him he was my best friend whom I am always talking about. My dad just sat there with a slight smirk on his face and snapped back, "Looks like somebody loves somebody."

I laughed and said, "No, we are just friends."

My mother wasn't there that evening. She was at the hospital with her baby sister, who was battling stage 4 cancer, but the rest of my family was. They all spoke to him and watched us both interact together.

After the party, I had Robert drive me home to get my car so I could run up to the Baptist hospital to visit my aunt. My aunt Phyliss was like my second mother. I was extremely close to her, and she always loved to hear my sister and me sing. Jennifer and I decided at the cookout that we would meet up there and just sing to her to lift her spirits some.

Once I arrived, Jennifer and her husband, Sam, were already there in the room, sitting on the wide windowsill. As I was settling into the room, Sam asked me about Robert, how we met, etc. My sister spoke up and asked me why we weren't dating. That seemed to be the running question of the night. Like my response all night, I stated, "We are just friends."

Later the next day, I jokingly told Robert about all that was said, and he laughed and agreed, "No, we are just friends." That never stopped my family from nudging me to look at him deeper, but I just couldn't. I couldn't seem to let go of the other man in my heart. I cried so many nights wondering where had I gone wrong, so I started praying more for direction and guidance.

I decided it was time I became more faithful to church, and I started attending Woodland Baptist Church in Rural Hall. I became a member there in September 2016. My parents had moved their membership there a few years prior, so I felt it only logical to go and be with my family.

While attending the services there, I started to feel that tug in my spirit again that I felt on my first date to the revival meeting. This tug surprised me. Why do I keep feeling this way? I know I am saved, and I have been baptized, yet that void of loneliness just got deeper and deeper.

During one of the sermons, I was asking myself why I feel so lost and feel like I hear God, but I keep finding myself wrong in the message I think I am receiving. I wanted a Christian man to love me and serve God with me. Why was that so hard for God to give me? What was I not doing right?

I went back in my mind to all my teachings that we as Christians should do. Tithing—that's it! I am not tithing. I need to give back to God. I started to give 10 percent of my gross pay plus another 5–10 percent as my offering. I was in my Bible more than I have ever been. At times, I felt God spoke to me when I did, but for the most part, reading my Bible felt as if I was reading a foreign language. I couldn't understand anything, except what I had been taught in the Bible when I was growing up. Nevertheless,

I never gave up. I kept reading, praying, and worshipping God.

There were times that I felt and knew God answered some of my prayers. I believe today that though I wasn't saved, because I worshiped God and credited to Him my blessings in life, God did hear and answer some of my prayers. But I was still very lost and on my way to hell and didn't even see it.

Fast forward, Robert and I continued to grow in our friendship. We started this new thing. Well, he added me in on his hobby. If we had a tough day or needed to blow steam, we went to the gun range for some "recoil therapy" as he called it. Robert was a huge firearm enthusiast. On our first trip together to the range, I remember thinking, *Who is this man, Rambo?* He had an entire armory with him. He introduced me to this beautiful Benelli rifle that he first taught me how to shoot along with several SIG Sauer pistols.

I remember him being so patient with me as I got used to handling a gun and as I felt that power that ran through my body after I took my first shot, missing the target completely. He gracefully would cheer me on while giving me tips on how to better aim and hit my target. We went to the range at least once a week, it seemed like, and I grew to love "recoil therapy" as much as he did. More than that, I began to appreciate the friendship that we were forming. Robert showed me he cared for me, and he always had my back and took care of me.

One day, he called me and said, "Hey, Momma, how would you like to see a Clemson game live at their stadium?" I told him that would be amazing. He informed me that some friends of his were going to go and tailgate before the game, and he wanted me to tag along. I thought it sounded awesome, so I was happy to accept.

When we arrived, none of his friends were there. And looking back, I am not sure anyone had truly planned to go. He never called to see where anyone was at or when they would be arriving. We focused on each other and had a great time.

After we got our bellies full, he was ready for a nap. We hopped in his truck, and he had a DVD player attached to his radio system. He put in his favorite movie, *Top Gun*. He got through the first ten minutes of it before I heard snoring from his side of the truck. I continued to watch the movie, then suddenly, the sky fell out. It started raining cats and dogs, the temperature dropped, and he woke up just in time to make our way to the stadium for the game to start.

There were so many people there. It was difficult to maneuver through the crowd without getting separated. Robert grabbed my hand and held on to it tightly as he created a path through the crowd to escort me to our seats. I remember that moment so vividly. It hit me kind of funny. Occasionally, even though he was holding so tightly to my hand, he would turn around to look at me to make sure I was okay. I felt something at that moment for him that I had never felt before. I saw him differently.

Once we got to our seats, I was drenched from head to toe. I wasn't dressed for rain. I had on jeans, a T-shirt, and his Clemson hoodie. It was freezing and cold, but I wasn't bothered by it. The game started, and the energy that surround the stadium as the Tigers ran down their hill to enter the field was just invigorating.

During the game, the rain picked up even more. By this time, I was so drenched that water from my hoodie was pouring down my face as if I had a water hose pointed directly at me. I was freezing, teeth chattering, but I was just so caught up in the energy of that night. I was so happy to just be there and to be in the company that I was with. Robert looked down at me as we stood up to cheer on the boys. I remember he looked at me with this oddly happy yet bewildered look on his face. I just smiled at him, and he wrapped his arm around me, and we both just started cheering on our team.

After the game, we had to walk back to the truck, which was a pretty good distance away from the stadium. It was still pouring the rain. And we were drenched. Once we got back to the truck, he dug into a duffel bag that he had in the back seat and pulled out some dry clothes that he had. He changed, and all he left was a very oversized T-shirt. I took it. It was like a dress on me, and I wasn't about to get sick from sitting in cold, wet clothes on the drive back to North Carolina.

He was extremely tired and tossed me the keys and asked me to drive us back home because he didn't feel he would make it, so I did. We arrived back at his apartment in the early hours of the morning, and he refused to let me drive home after not sleeping at all. I crashed on his couch for a few hours and then went home.

A few days later, Robert asked me an odd off-the-wall question: "Have you ever felt that you have always known something, but you didn't know it until it slapped you in the face?"

I laughed and looked at him, busting out with the word *no*. He stood there in silence for a few seconds, so I asked him why he asked me that. As he shifted from one side to the other, he said that when we were at the game, he looked down at me and saw how soaking wet I was, and he knew I had to be freezing, yet I was smiling and just happy to be there and to be with him that I never complained, not once. He looked me in my eyes and said, "That's when it slapped me in my face."

I asked him what hit him.

"That I am in love with you."

My mind suddenly recalled the memory of the emotions that hit me that very same night as he was guiding me through the crowds and was so protective over me in making sure I was okay. All I could think to myself was, *No, no, no, we are best friends. I don't want to risk ruining that.* I told him this and how I felt like I had looked at him differently that night as well, but did we want to take that risk and possibly ruin what we had?

We had agreed years ago that we were best suited as friends. He agreed for like a week. I had committed to a date with a guy that he knew. I had asked him the night before the date if there was anything I should know about this guy, and he told me he was a stand-up, conservative guy as far as he knew.

That entire next day, he was freaking out. He kept calling me and asking me if I wanted to meet this guy. He would throw things at me that made no sense at all just to derail me from going. I found out later that he called his best friend and told him he didn't understand why, but he was just sick on his stomach over my going on this date. I went on the date, and all I could think about was Robert the entire time, so needless to say, that date amounted to nothing more than a nice dinner.

A few days later, Robert and I agreed to take the risk and date. It didn't take him very long before he started flirting with the idea of marriage. I thought, *Finally, God has sent me the man I have prayed for so long, and he has been right here under my nose this entire time.*

A year later, out of nowhere, it was in the middle of the afternoon. He had just gotten home from work, and I had been there cleaning his house. I had just finished making his bed after washing his bedding. He came in and immediately cluttered it all up with papers and junk. I sat there to help him once I realized he decided to clean out his nightstand.

As I was sitting in the middle of the bed, he lay across it and was reading receipts that he was trying to figure out if he should trash or keep. While we were just chatting about stuff, he randomly started getting supersweet with his conversation. He told me that I was the best friend that he has ever had, that I was special. He explained that he felt that he would always be a bachelor because to him, marriage was the ultimate commitment. He felt once married, there was no going back. He held his parents' forty-three-year marriage in high regard on what a marriage should be and that he had never met a girl who made him feel like she was worthy of that role till now.

He looked over at me and so sincerely told me that the moment he met me, he knew there was something different about me, that no matter how he tried, he never could stop thinking about me throughout his days, that he knew if anything were to ever happen to him, I would be the woman who would have his back and would be by his side through it all. He told me how much he had grown to love me.

Robert looked at me and said, "Well, I hadn't planned to do this yet, but it just seems right. I would be so honored if you would marry me."

I couldn't believe it. This was the man whom I have heard say time and time again that marriage was not for him, and he is now asking me to marry him. I didn't even have to think about it. I knew I loved him. We had the best relationship. We created a bond over a friendship that would last a lifetime. What better than to marry your best friend. I agreed to marry him.

We set our date to be married on January 7, 2019. That year went by quickly. We had a small ceremony at the small white chapel in Tanglewood Park. We didn't have an ordained pastor available to us because we were getting married on Monday, so before the scheduled ceremony, he and I, along with our parents and photographer, met at the local courthouse of Mocksville, and we were married by the justice of the peace. Then we parted ways to prepare for our formal wedding ceremony. My brother-in-law Sam officiated the ceremony for us. The wedding was intimate, with select friends and family. It was perfect for us. We later were blessed to spend our honeymoon in Maui thanks to his wonderful, loving parents, Walt and Sherry.

Once we arrived back home, we were on a mission to purchase our first home together. We searched and viewed house after house and applied offer after offer just to lead to continuous disappointment. I began to get frustrated. I turned to God. I started praying and begging God to lead us to the home He had for us, but months went by with nothing in our favor. I wasn't as faithful to church as I had been before, so I felt that was hindering me from having my prayers heard. But I stayed faithful in my prayers for a home.

Later, in July, we found a brand-new construction home in the city limits of my hometown of Mocksville. It was just within the mileage for Robert to be able to bring his work truck home. It was eight minutes from my child-hood home where my parents still live and eight minutes from my sister and twelve minutes from my brother. It was a bit farther from his parents and his job, but Robert said that it didn't bother him. He loved the home and could see himself living there. I was trying not to get attached because I had already been let down so many times. We took the night to think on it, and the next morning, he called our relator and put in an offer a little above pricing, and it was accepted immediately. We closed on August 9, 2019.

CHAPTER 4

Answered Prayers or God's Design?

Newly married to the man whom I never saw coming. Robert and I had been best friends for five years now, and I never expected in my wildest dreams that he would be the one whom I would marry. We had such a strong bond. That man had my back on everything in life. He was protective not just over me physically, but he was protective of my heart. Robert could come across as a little awkward and quiet to those who didn't know him, but he had the biggest heart and such a strong, dry sense of humor. We were on the level of knowing what each other was thinking before we ever had to say it. He truly was my best friend.

Here it was, 2019, and we had just begun a new chapter in our lives—married on January 7, 2019, and then purchased our first home together as husband and wife in August. Everything was seemingly perfect. Finally, I had that healthy, loving, consistent relationship with a man who was saved and believed as I did.

Robert not only loved me, but he also loved my two children. Not having any children of his own, he stepped into that role of fatherhood with pride and open arms to my children. Emma and Riley have a great relationship with their dad, but they were also able to bond with Robert in a way that made me so proud. Emma quickly became the daughter that Robert always wanted, and he spoiled her. He never knew how to tell that little girl no. She would be so happy when he arrived home from work that she would run out the door as soon as she heard his truck pull up and greet him with the biggest hug. He squeezed her and looked up at the door to where I would be standing and just beam from ear to ear. He ate it up.

He and Riley had a much different relationship. They understood each other in a way that words were rarely needed. Robert tried to take Riley up under his wing and tried to teach him things that Riley would one day benefit from once he reached adulthood.

Robert took the time to always take notice of our children and their body language each day. He could always tell if they were happy or unhappy, and he took the time to sit down with them and gave them his shoulder. He would always approach my children with love and acceptance, allowing them the security they needed to feel they could open up to him, and he would listen. There were several times that my children felt more comfortable talking to Robert than they did with me or their dad. He created a bond with them that most stepparents are too intimidated to try. He was the light that shined in our world.

I could share so many other stories of the wonderful relationship that we all had within the four walls of the Wall residence. But even with it being nearly the life most dream to have, it didn't come without its hiccups. We all are human, and we all will fail at some point or another, and we had our share of disagreements, our battling the parenting side of the same situations that any parent will face in life. But we were all very happy.

Somehow, having all of this, I still felt deep inside that void that something was missing, and this whole time, I thought it was Mr. Right. Well, now he is here, but the void is still there, and the depth is just as deep. What could be missing?

I sat out in my heart to analyze this thing and fix it. I was so tired of being lonely. I had the best relationship, I had the best two kids a woman could ask for, I had a beautiful home, I had a beautiful car, we have taken amazing trips together, and even had a huge family trip to Atlantis coming up. Why in the world was I feeling this way? I had no right to feel this way.

Days passed, and I just kept on living my life. I decided that maybe it was my Bible reading. It wasn't a daily occurrence, so I decided to try to read it more. There were some weeks I remained faithful and some weeks it never got picked up. One day, I mentioned to Robert that I felt we needed to be more faithful to church because I had gotten in a habit of not going as much, and when I did, it was only on Sunday mornings. Robert agreed that we should find a church home and be faithful.

At this time, my dad had just become the pastor of Lighthouse Baptist Church in Lexington, North Carolina. It was about a thirty-five-minute drive from our home. Robert mentioned going there. Robert admired my dad. He always told me how much my dad meant to him and how he felt like my dad was someone he looked up to and had great respect for.

The following Sunday, we got up and dressed and drove out to my dad's church and surprised him and my mother. We came faithfully for about a month, then we decided to join and make Lighthouse our home church.

As we started to be faithful in church, Robert's heart became more tender to things of the Lord. You see, Robert was saved at the age of fourteen while on a trip to Bible camp. But when Robert reached adulthood, he attended his home church on Sunday mornings, and that was about it, and even then, it was as faithful as he would have liked. He had told me once before in the years of our budding friendship that he struggled with the idea of having to be in church all the time. At one point he felt called to be a pastor, but he never pursued it. He and I shared countless conversations about the Bible, heaven, and our viewpoints on the Christian life throughout our relationship in knowing each other.

Robert had so many questions. I remember on the car ride home after a Sunday-morning service, Robert told me how much he loved to hear my dad preach, how much he loved my dad. He mentioned that he wanted to go to breakfast with him some morning just so he could pick his brain and ask all the questions that he had regarding the Bible and God. He began to get a little emotional and mentioned that my dad was such an inspiration to him. He felt that my dad would be a good influence on him. I didn't have anything to say. I sat there with pride in my heart that my husband felt this way toward my dad.

All the while Robert's heart was growing more curious and tender, mine was growing more anxious and confused. I had questions too, but they weren't the same as his. I felt I knew God. I felt I knew my Bible. I mean, after all, I grew up with it all being ingrained into me. I could quote you scripture from all the years of having to memorize them. I knew God. I could tell you all about Him. I mean, after all, He did just answer my biggest prayer of finding me the man I was praying for, right?

I later found myself telling Robert one night lying in bed how I was feeling. I was crying because I felt so broken. He held my hand and listened intently as I told him that I know I have no reason in the world to feel this way, but I felt so alone. Even in a crowd full of people, I felt unnoticed and alone. I knew I had him and my kids, and I was so thankful for it, but this void was just overwhelming and unshakable. He compassionately asked me that if I felt like I was in my Bible more, would it help? And I told him no. I felt like I don't understand it even though I try so hard to, but maybe God will help me eventually.

Days passed by, and weeks turned into a few months. Christmastime was coming, the best time of the year for me typically. But this year, it wasn't that way in my heart. I was battling my health. I was gaining weight like crazy. No matter how hard I tried to keep my weight down, it kept gaining. I was miserable. I was starting to feel that it was affecting the way my husband looked at me even though he tried to keep me positive. I beat myself up and down every day.

I was starting to feel that segregated feeling from my family again. It always seems like this feeling has been there in the shadows my entire life. I always felt overlooked by my family. I never saw or spoke to any of them unless they wanted or needed me for something or I made the effort to go to them, and then my time spent with them was spent listening to their happy or disgruntled emotions toward another family member.

I felt so invisible. I felt it even reflected onto my children. They rarely have spent time with my side of the family unless it was large family events that everyone showed up to. *No* family is perfect. We all have our pitfalls because we are all human beings, and well, it happens. I tried to tell myself that all the time, but it never seemed to help.

I later told Robert that I felt maybe this was the cause of the void I was always feeling. The only family members that I ever felt took time to cheer me on in my achievements or put the effort in to hug me when I failed or seemed to be kicked down were my sister Jennifer and my aunt Phyliss.

Now please don't misread what I am telling you. I have a wonderful family. I have amazing parents who sacrificed everything to make sure their children had the things they needed in life. I just was the strong-willed, stubborn, opinionated middle child. I was the child who took nothing off people and had no filter in my mouth and would easily call someone out, and most of the time, it was not in a gracious, loving way. I am a fighter. I will stand up for what I believe, and I will fight till my last breath for the ones whom I love. But when it comes to myself, I tend to take a back seat.

I have told my mother several times how I felt, and the response was always, "You know we love you. You are our child, and I thank God for you every day. I just know you are a strong woman, and you don't need my help. Your dad and I don't feel we need to worry about you like we do your other siblings."

That may sound like a compliment, but it didn't take to me as one. That just kicked me even further down. I know the things I have faced in my life, things that most people fortunately never have to, but I did, and yes, I have managed to pick myself up and keep moving because I am built strong and I am a fighter. I was a mother. I had no choice. I had little ones who needed me, but I needed someone too.

I went home feeling even more alone. I felt so unworthy of love. It created jealousy in my heart toward my other siblings. But somehow, with my sister's continuance of kindness and support, I never could stay bitter toward her. Jennifer saw exactly how I felt, and she could see the things happening that would make me feel the way that I did. Because of that, she pulled me in and loved me even harder.

Jennifer herself was facing some of the hardest times in her life. But even when she was down, she picked me up, and I feel that is because God was using her compassionate heart to keep me close. I had so many dark forces trying to destroy me. The events that I have faced in life should have destroyed me, should have beaten me down to a place so low in my life that I shouldn't be able to hold my head up. Somehow, between her and the love of my aunt Phyliss and then Robert being brought into my life, I was able to keep fighting one day at a time. My aunt Phyliss is in heaven today. She was my mom's baby sister. She passed away at the young age of fifty-six by the hand of cancer.

Phyliss was like my second mother. Not only did I favor her and carried a lot of her personality traits, but my life story had many similarities to hers. She was able to talk me off my ledge more times than I could count. There were countless nights before she got sick that I would call her at three or four in the morning, and she always picked up the call. Phyliss faced even more in her lifetime than I did, and that woman never let it stop her.

She went on to make something of herself, and she made a positive name for herself. She showed me so much grace and compassion. She helped me understand that life isn't always rainbows and butterflies, that sometimes it was cold and dark, but we had to keep on walking. When I felt like giving up, she kept pushing me to move. For that, I will always be eternally grateful.

Even with the love and support of these three amazing people in my life, that void continued to grow deeper.

CHAPTER 5

Storm Clouds Gathering

January 29, 2020

Robert turned thirty-nine years old. The year had come in like a wrecking ball. The talk was just beginning to buzz around about this new virus called corona hitting our country. Robert's company was just bought out from another brand. His work was steady. I was trying to get my own new business up and running. Life was busy but seemed good.

With all that was going on, everyone was so busy. We never got a chance to properly celebrate Robert's birthday, and his parents wanted to take us to dinner to celebrate. By this time, it was already the middle of February. It was cold and slightly raining that night. He had chosen Ichiban Japanese in Salisbury to meet his parents. He rushed home from work, showered, and got dressed. He had been battling some strange symptoms for several months now. That entire day and evening was one of the worst days for his feeling sickly. He didn't feel like he wanted to do anything but go to bed, but he didn't want to let his parents down, so he decided to fight through it a little bit longer.

On our way there, I could tell he was feeling sick. He was struggling to see the road and complained of a massive headache. He pulled over halfway there and made me change seats with him so that I could drive us there safely. Once we arrived, he put his best face forward and tried to hide the fact he wasn't feeling great. Once we were seated around the grill and got settled in, we could finally hear each other talk. The cook had already come out and started cooking our food. Yummy! Chicken, steak, shrimp, rice, zucchini. Oh, how the cook started talking in my language. He had already placed everyone's portion of rice and veggies on our plates, and my father-in-law was trying to teach this klutz how to use chopsticks. Sorry, Walt, still not that great with them.

Robert just ate and stayed a little quiet as we all talked. Then out of nowhere, his arm comes sweeping around, just barely missing the side of my face. I immediately turned in shock. "What in the world is wrong with you?" thinking he just tried to hit me. And as I was able to turn my body around to get a good look at him, I noticed his body was slumped in his chair. He was convulsing so violently, and his poor lips were turning blue. Robert was having his very first grand mal seizure.

I was feeling the adrenaline to help him, but I didn't know how. I just held on to him to keep him from hurting himself. Fortunately, there were five paramedics in the opposite room eating their supper. They were able to take over the situation and help him. Once he came to, he had no idea what had happened or where he was. We chose to go on and load him up on the ambulance, and from there, he was transported to the nearby hospital.

No one could explain why this happened. However, they did remove one medication he was on to help him stop his tobacco use. Wellbutrin helps thousands of people each year over the bad habit of tobacco use. However, there is a risk that comes with that drug. If you are someone who has a low threshold for seizures, well. this drug will catapult you into them.

Robert, though never diagnosed with seizures before, has been suspected over the last ten years to have been having episodes of absence seizures. Absence seizures are where someone would just pause, seem to be staring off into space. Some can have rapid blinking. Robert had a few times in his life where the staring off into space had happened. He would come to and be a little confused and not know what he was doing, but he just ignored it, thinking it was nothing.

After that seizure, Robert was placed on a medical layoff. He couldn't drive for six months. His entire job depended on his driving a truck every day. This now meant he couldn't work for six months. The new owner of the company called Robert directly and extended so much grace and kindness to him, assuring him that he cared about his well-being and that he wanted him to not worry about his job status, to take the time to help himself, and his job would be there waiting on him when he got back. They offered him a short-term disability to help him during this time.

By this time, corona, or as we now refer to as COVID-19, was starting to make its way across our country. Quarantine was being put into place. People were being laid off from jobs or quitting their jobs, and people were being told to not leave their homes unless it was an emergency.

My new business was taking a hard hit. I was forced to close my doors. During this time, though I didn't understand it, it was a blessing in disguise. I was able to be home every day for six solid months. Believe it or not, instead of our getting to a point of being sick of each other, we became even closer. We enjoyed our time together.

Unfortunately, when Robert had to see his physician for his follow-up after his hospital visit, his doctor did something to this day I still question why. He put him right back on Wellbutrin, knowing that the neurologist took him off it, believing it was the reason his seizure episodes turned so violent. We sat in his office and asked him if that was wise. He laughed and said, it's not going to hurt him. If he was feeling good about it and it was helping him, then it will not harm him. *What a joke.*

That first week of starting it back in his system, Robert had two strong seizures back-to-back. We placed him in the hospital once again. This time, Wellbutrin was being taken off his medicine list for good.

As the months passed by, Robert started to feel a little more like himself, wasn't a seizure in sight. He started feeling so good and happy that he decided to plan another trip to Maui while we had this time off together. Unfortunately,

COVID-19 prevented that trip from happening in June like he wanted, so he moved it to our second wedding anniversary date. Why not? It is where we honeymooned.

As time kept going by, things with the virus seemed to be improving, and quarantine was being lifted in small amounts. My family decided we all wanted to go to the beach, so we all hit Airbnb and found two beach condos to house us all at Folly Beach on Hilton Head Island. It was the last week of July, and I had found a weight-loss program that was working great for me. I had dropped thirty-five pounds in two months, and I believed in it so much, I invested in the company and became a certified health coach.

That week, I was making some extra income coaching. I was with my family, my husband was feeling great, my kids were having a blast, and we were able to reconnect with my parents and my sister and her family. We had the best week.

Once we arrived back home, Robert had to prepare to go on another week's stay, but this time, it wasn't for fun. He was scheduled the very following week to be admitted into the hospital for an epilepsy study. That week, his mother and I took turns sitting with him to help keep him awake. The doctors didn't want him to get any sleep for three days. Their goal was to hopefully trigger a seizure from sleep deprivation in hopes that they could monitor him and see where the seizure originated from and hopefully see what was causing them. Their plan was successful. On the fourth night, he went into a seizure.

They were able to locate where they started. They mentioned that though they couldn't exactly determine the cause, they could tell that his electric currents in that part of his brain were not firing off properly, so we were having to face more and more doctor visits.

Robert has scheduled a September appointment for a follow-up visit with his neurologist to come up with a treatment plan to help at least try to prevent them from happening. Over the weeks, Robert would have great days then not so many good days. He always complained of a terrible headache. He ate Tylenol like candy.

One night, we had gone over to his parents' home for supper. He wasn't feeling great again, and his mother noticed and kept asking him if he was okay. He kept assuring her that he was fine, but he wasn't. His eyes were very dilated and glassy. When we arrived back home that evening, he had gotten worse. His eyes looked so strange to me. He was weak and just in pain with that horrible headache. I made him come inside, and I don't know why, but I told him I felt we needed to check his blood pressure.

Every time Robert had a seizure, it was accompanied by extremely high blood pressure, which his doctors again decided not to treat. They just told him to stop eating salt and walk. I believe the massive headaches were a symptom of his blood pressure being high all the time.

Once we got inside the house, I dug out the blood pressure cuff, and sure enough, his blood pressure was very high. He wouldn't go to the hospital, so I asked him if he wouldn't listen to me, at least let me call the nurses' line on our medical insurance and get their opinion if he should go or not, and if they felt it wasn't alarming for him to go, then I wouldn't make him go. He agreed to that.

I called and was able to speak to a nurse. I told him of his history. I informed him of his behavior that evening that led me to check his blood pressure. She asked for his readings when I checked it and then had me do it again with her on the line. The second time, it had increased even more from the first time, and she told me to get him to the emergency immediately and not to take no for an answer from him. She was on speakerphone, and Robert just started to get dressed because he knew he wasn't staying home.

Once we arrived at the hospital, they ushered him in immediately. They pumped him full of meds to bring his pressure back down. They ran him through scans and did the test. This doctor checked him very thoroughly, unlike any of the other doctors he had seen prior. She noticed that his right eye was limited in its range of movement, which concerned her. She was worried that he may have had a small stroke then, and it just hadn't shown up on the scan. She urged him to follow up with his neurologist immediately. So the very next day, I made all the calls to get him scheduled to see his doctor.

Once we were able to see his neurologist, Robert explained everything to him about how he feels from day to day. We passed him the notes from the ER doctor, and I'll never forget it as long as I live. His doctor leaned over, braced his arms on his knees. and placed and locked his hands together. He looked at Robert and said, "Mr. Wall, I have all your test results here in front of me, and yes, we have evidence of your seizures. I don't feel a cause to be alarmed. I feel the treatment we have in place for you will be what is best.

"However, Mr. Wall, life gets hard sometimes, and we are human. Depression is a real thing. I feel your best route right now will be to find a great therapist or psychiatrist who might be able to help you sort through this depression you seem to have."

What? Did I just hear him correctly? Did I just hear this doctor tell my husband his problem was depression? You have got to be kidding me. Robert just kind of looked over at me, raised his eyebrows, and then hung his head, as if to tell me, "This is the reason I don't go to doctors. They don't listen."

My heart broke into a million pieces. I couldn't keep quiet. I got upset and emotional and looked at that doctor. I told him, "Excuse me. What he is telling you is not depression. He may feel low because he feels defeated in his healthcare. I live with this man, so it isn't just his words when I tell you that I witness this with him daily. It isn't normal how he is. There is something extremely wrong with him. I am afraid that one day, I am going to find my husband dead."

His doctor had nothing more to say other than, "Here is a psychiatrist that I will be recommending to you."

Well, to keep anyone from saying he didn't try to help himself, Robert made the appointment and saw the psychiatrist. Her findings were that he was normal and had no signs of depression.

CHAPTER 6

The Shaking of Hallowed Ground

Fall is here. The weather is slightly beginning to change, leaves are changing, and cooler weather is blowing in. Weeks have gone by since Robert had seen the psychiatrist. He was finally back at work and settling back into his normal routine. Robert loved his job. He loved being in a truck and working with his hands every day. He was happy to be getting somewhat back to normal.

Robert was not one to sit still. He was what I like to call a *piddler*. He always had to be messing with something. He enjoyed working in the yard and messing around in the garage. If he ever sat down, you could bet your bottom dollar he would be snoring within ten minutes. Curling up with him to watch a movie together was never an option. Occasionally, I might get a few shows of his favorite TV series, but even those could not hold him down before he would be up digging in drawers, messing with something. His mind was always all over the place.

Things seemed like they were improving. He found the entire month of October that he had some amazingly strong energy burst. He told me at one point that he hadn't felt that great in years. We were starting to be hopeful that whatever he had been experiencing was finally on its way out the door. He just wanted to feel whole and like a man again, and he was getting there.

Everything was great on the home front. However, I was still battling that feeling of loneliness that I just couldn't shake. I started to think for a time that maybe it was because of battling Robert's health and getting no answers that I was feeling this way. Robert loved me with a strong love, and he held me on a pedestal that even sometimes made me feel worried that I wouldn't be able to always live up to it.

Our relationship was strong, and we shared a bond from the tightest of friendships. Because we were so close, that allowed ease and comfort in communicating with one another. We always knew how to approach each other and how to listen and speak when needed. Robert allowed me his shoulder to cry on numerous times. I was feeling so worried for him, and he would express his concerns as well.

Now that everything seems to be improving, I felt I could turn to him as I have for years. My best friend—I needed to talk to my best friend. I opened up to him once again about everything we were going through. On top of that, I was still battling my very deep emotions of feeling segregated from my own family. I didn't feel close to them. I felt I couldn't talk to them, and if I did, I felt I was never heard. I felt that when I did speak, they would always talk over me or make it all about them or someone else, and the subject would be dropped. I felt alone. I felt I didn't matter. I felt I only heard from my family when they wanted something. Satan was in my ears constantly, telling me that I meant nothing to them. I felt like the redheaded stepchild.

November 6, 2020

Robert and I took the children out for a nice dinner, then we came home, and he messed around in the garage for a couple of hours. I cleaned up the kitchen and then decided to retreat into a hot bath. A few hours later, the kids disappeared to their rooms, and Robert and I retired to our room to watch a few episodes of *Longmire* before going to bed.

That night, Robert seemed spacey after dinner. We figured it was like all the other times. His blood pressure was probably spiking. He complained of a bad headache and asked me if I would massage his head. For those of you who didn't know Robert, he had the prettiest, shiniest bald noggin. I kept essential oils on hand and had a bottle of peppermint oil, and I used that to massage his head. He didn't make it through the first episode and was out like a light.

I made sure he was covered, turned the TV off, and washed the oil off my hands, then I went and crawled into my side of the bed and dozed off. That night, I had a series of dreams about the issues I felt I had with my family. I tossed and turned all night.

That next morning, November 7, I woke up angry. I was crying and just in a bad mood. Robert decided that we needed to do something with the kids and get our minds off everything. I agreed but not before I word vomited all over him with tears rolling down my face. I exclaimed that I was done. I was cutting ties with my family. I didn't deserve to feel like the black sheep of my family, that I was so tired of feeling like I had to compete with my brother and his wife or my sister and her boys, that I was just done.

Robert hugged me so tight at that moment. He kept drying the tears that were streaming down my face. He pulled me into him and told me, "Hunni, don't do that. I understand why you feel the way you do. I see it myself, but I truly don't think any of it is on purpose. I know for a fact your parents love you. Hunni, don't give up on them."

I continued to cry as I pushed away from him and told him no. I was done. He came closer to me and pulled me into his chest. He whispered in my ear, "I love you. You are my entire world, and I could never live this life without you. I hope you know that and know I will always have your back."

I held him tight as the tears fell, and I told him I knew he loved me, and I was thankful that I at least had him and my children.

We changed the subject and decided we were going to make the best of that day and have a blast with the kids. He decided that I should take Emma to the spa and have a girls' day. He would take Riley to Mooresville to the go-cart track, and they would enjoy just being boys with their toys for the day. He started running around and messing in everything, trying to get a few things done before they left. I had to shower and get ready still.

After I had showered, Robert came in to check on how much longer I had before I was ready to go. I told him that I still had roughly thirty minutes to finish my makeup and hair and throw some clothes on. He proceeded to inform me that Riley wanted to shower before they left, so he was tinkering around on his motorcycle and wanted to change the oil on it. He needed to run up to the store above our house to grab the oil that he needed and would be back before Emma and I left. He gave me a quick kiss and jetted out the door.

I continued to finish up my routine of getting dressed. Thirty minutes passed, and I was ready to go. I walked out of my room to make sure Emma was dressed and ready and noticed Robert hadn't arrived back home yet. I told Riley that he should have been back by now, so he would more than likely be returning soon and to just sit tight and keep the doors locked. Little did I know that my hallowed ground was about to be shaken.

Emma and I entered the garage, and she was already making her way into the car. I raised the garage door and noticed Robert had moved his car in a strange position, and it was blocking my car from exiting the garage. I assumed he had taken his truck to the store, and I was agitated as to why he would just leave his car like that.

I began to look on the tool chest for his car keys so I could move the car, and they were not hanging where he generally keeps them. I thought, *Well, he must have left them in the car.* I began to walk toward the car and noticed he was in it. I was hollering at him, "Robert, what are you doing? I need to get out. Could you please move the car?" and he didn't acknowledge me.

I approached the car closer and opened the door. "Babe, what in the world are you doing?" When I opened the door, he was slumped over the middle console on the passenger side. I grabbed his arm, asking him if he was okay. He was heavy. It took everything in me to pull him upward.

Once he was sitting straight, his head hung low, and I lifted his face and saw no life in his eyes. His lips were blue. I then noticed the vomit on his face and his clothes. It appeared he had soiled his pants. I immediately knew he had seized. I pulled him out of the car and got him on the ground, hollering at Emma to call 911. She didn't know why and came running up and saw her stepdad was lifeless on the driveway. I was panicking, screaming for any neighbor of mine to help. Normally, the yards were full of people at that time of day on a Saturday, but that morning, it was silent.

Emma had a dispatcher on the phone. She remained so calm and tried her best to give the lady the information that she asked for. I, on the other hand, was frantic. I was giving him CPR and couldn't see a sign of life. Then out of nowhere, one of my neighbors from up the street, Jason Cibelli, immediately took over the chest compressions so I could talk to the dispatcher. He was like an angel who appeared out of nowhere. He worked what seemed like ten to fifteen minutes on him till the paramedics arrived. Once they arrived, he went and grabbed my children and wrapped his arms around them both and kept them out of view of what going on with Robert. All I could do at that moment was fall to the bumper of the back of Robert's car, begging God to save him. I immediately apologized for everything and begged God to please not take my husband.

The paramedics came with a machine that did the compressions for them. It was the only one in all of Davie County, and this truck just so happened to have been the one that had it. They immediately got that thing on him as five men worked hard to get him breathing again. It felt like hours going by. I had called both my parents, and my mom didn't answer. My dad took my call, and I just remember yelling at him that I needed him now. Robert was found dead, and I needed him here.

My dad was where he is every weekend: out soul-winning and visiting his church members. He was out in Denton, North Carolina, at least an hour away. I called my sister, and she was at work but dropped all she was doing and was headed my way. She was still a half hour away. Here I was, alone and scared out of my mind. I walked over to my children and grabbed them and just started singing "Jesus Is the Sweetest Name I Know."

After I stopped singing, I walked back to where Robert was, still not having gotten any sign of life. The paramedics were running off pure adrenaline and arguing with one another because they were just all trying to help him but were getting in each other's way.

I turned around, and arms wrapped around me. No words were spoken, just a strong, tight, comforting grip embraced me. I looked up into the most piercing blue eyes that were filled with what looked like the deep pain my own heart was feeling. Those eyes were the eyes of the one person I found myself the angriest toward, the person I felt I couldn't live up to, the person I was ready to cut out of my life. That person was my brother. When no one else could get there or be there, Perry was the one. My dad called my sister-in-law Lauren, she barely could relay to my brother details of what was happening before he jumped in his truck and was at my home in no time.

I just remember feeling so ashamed at that moment of how I felt earlier that morning. It was like God whispered, "Your family loves you." I truly felt that day that Perry felt my pain as deeply as I did. I'll never forget that strong grip of love that I felt that day when he grabbed me and squeezed me.

Just a few minutes passed as everyone was starting to gather in my yard. We all saw Robert being rolled to his side as he vomited and struggled to catch his breath. The paramedics worked quickly to make sure he was going to keep breathing. He finally started to breathe on his own. Thank You, Lord.

They loaded him up on the gurney and got him on the truck. They rushed him to Forsyth Hospital as I had to stay behind to answer a police officer's questions concerning the events that happened. My sister-in-law gathered Robert's medications as another paramedic placed Robert's wedding band and watch in my hands.

At that moment, my mind shut down. Everything started to be like a dream. This wasn't happening to me. I had to make that difficult phone call to Walt and Sherry. They planned to meet me at the hospital. I remember my sister driving me there, and the entire ride was just pure shock. All I could recall in my mind was the fact just two months ago, I pleaded with his doctor and stated my worst fear was to find him dead one day. I had no idea it was going to be as soon as it was. This was not happening to me.

Once I arrived at the emergency room, I informed the nurse at the desk who I was. I no more got my last name out of my mouth than she jumped up out of her seat and said, "Mrs. Wall, please follow me." She escorted me down the hall till we finally came to a small room that was designated for families of critical patients.

As I entered the room, my in-laws were already there. They greeted me with a hug and a sense of worry. Robert is their only child. I knew as his wife how hard this was worrying me. I couldn't even begin to know what they were feeling as well.

As we sat in there on pins and needles, waiting to just hear something, we tried to keep the spirit light and hopeful. The ER doctor came in and explained that they had to medically paralyze him to keep him still in the MRI machine. He was struggling and continued to seize. They said that they were moving him up to the IC floor and that I should follow them up, and they would place me in a room to wait till the doctor could speak to me. During the COVID outbreak, I was the only one who was allowed to go upstairs at that time.

I was escorted through the large hospital. We finally reached the IC floor, and they opened a closed waiting room just for me to sit there and wait on the doctor. The staff was so respectful and kind. I walked over to the bench near the window.

After the nurse closed the door, I sat down and just began to feel that pit of loneliness and fear to a degree that was just unbearable. I looked at the window as tears began to stream down my face. Robert was the one thing that was always consistent in my life. He was my best friend, and now I may lose him. I couldn't wrap my head around it.

As I sat there praying and begging God to intervene, my phone rang. It was the doctor who was working with Robert. He informed me that this was not looking good, that Robert needed a ton of prayers. He told me that they were placing him in his room, and when he was settled, a nurse would come to get me, and I could see him.

It wasn't much longer and I was brought to his room. There was my best friend, my husband, lying there in that bed with hoses all in his face, IVs all in his arms and incoherent. I walked over and grabbed his hand and kissed his cheek and told him that I was there and that I loved him. I just squeezed his hand and wished I could just fix him. I wanted to take it all away. He was a man who would give anyone the shirt off his back. He had the biggest heart. He didn't deserve to be here like that.

They finally allowed his parents to join me in the room with him. We had no words. It was a room of silence and tears. None of us could wrap our minds around why this was happening. I sat there all day with him. My family was all there at the hospital downstairs outside. Due to the COVID rules and regulations, they were not allowed to wait inside the hospital.

That evening, the neurologist came to his room and discussed the plan of treatment for him. They were going to do a series of warming him up and cooling him down to try to eliminate the amount of swelling in his brain.

Robert was only thirty-nine years of age, and he had been without oxygen for a long time. Due to the fact he was so young, there was no room in his skull for the extra swelling. This was extremely dangerous to the quality of life that he would have.

As it got later, I asked my parents to take me home so I could shower and get some rest so I could remain strong for him. He needed me right now to be at my best. My parents took me home. My mom stayed with me as my dad went back to his home to take care of their dog, and he was going to attempt to get some sleep as well because he was facing having to get up in the pulpit the next morning and preach and have his church pray for Robert and the family.

After I got home and settled, I told my mom I felt helpless, that I needed to be doing something, so I read my Bible and prayed and prayed and prayed. I later felt I needed more prayers, so I logged into my Facebook account and went live. I began to explain what I was facing and just simply asked for everyone's prayers. Little did I know that video would locally go viral. I had thousands praying for us.

I started to doze off in the recliner. My mom was asleep on my couch. At 3:00 a.m. on November 8, 2020, the doctor called. He said, "Mrs. Wall, your husband is having a very difficult night. He keeps having seizures. We are doing all we can to keep him comfortable and to help him. He is never left alone. There is medical staff with him around the clock. Mrs. Wall, your husband needs a miracle. I will keep you posted on any new changes."

CHAPTER 7

The Awakening

November 8, 2020, at 3:20 a.m., I had just hung up the call from the hospital. Robert was in the biggest fight for his life. I was just told his odds were not in his favor, and he needed a miracle. A miracle? Well, I just so happen to know the miracle maker. I got myself up out of my chair in the dark and found my way to my ottoman. My mom was silently sitting on the couch, trying to soak in that call. I got on my knees and started crying out to God.

I prayed and cried, begging God to step in at any time now and revive Robert and heal him. The more I prayed, the deeper I felt that void, that pit of loneliness. Out of desperation, anger, and fear, I started to yell out to God, "*Where are You?* God, I am here. Now where are You? My whole life, I was taught from the Bible that You would never leave me or forsake me. *Where are You?*"

I was getting to feel that anger because it just kept feeling so cold and empty in that room. I was begging for my husband's life, I couldn't understand why God was not here. Why was He not listening to me? Then as I yelled even louder through my tears, "Where are You, God?" I suddenly felt overcome by a presence greater than myself. My prayers for Robert turned to the realization of why I felt alone: because I was alone.

God's voice spoke directly to my heart: "I don't know you."

I froze and was surprised. "What do You mean You don't know me? I grew up in a Christian home. I was raised in the church and Christian school. I said the Sinner's prayer when I was five years old. What do You mean You don't know me? I worshipped You. I have prayed to You. I tried to read my Bible daily. What do You mean You don't know me?"

At that moment, my entire life flashed before my eyes. I suddenly remembered everything I have ever done or said. I remembered the life of sin that I chose to live. I suddenly felt ashamed and asked for forgiveness.

That soft yet powerful voice rang in my ears once more: "Robert is going to be okay. However, you are lost and on your way to hell."

I sat there with tears streaming down my face. How in the world could I have been so blind, so deceived my entire life. I suddenly shifted my prayers from saving Robert to asking for forgiveness and asking God to save me. At that moment, He reached down in my darkest hour, within my deepest pain. He was able to lift me out and save my soul.

As the night passed, I finally made myself clean up and head back to the hospital to be with Robert. I sat by his side for hours until his parents could get there, and then I switched off with them to allow them their time with him as well. I went downstairs to find every single one of my family members was camped outside of that hospital with their lawn chairs. The family that I was going to cut ties with was all there.

God opened my eyes not only to the deception that Satan had over me concerning my salvation but the deception of lies he told me that my own family hated me. They all sat outside around me, praying with me and for God's will be done for Robert. We all were still clinging on to that hope that he would make it even though his chances didn't look good.

As the day went on, so many people reached out and let me know they were praying. Others brought us food and coffee. Everyone poured so much love onto me and my family. I returned to Robert's room and turned on Joy FM, a Christian radio station to fill his room with uplifting music. I could strongly feel the presence of God in that room. I hadn't a clue what was going on with Robert at this point. We were just sitting and waiting.

Later that night, things had not progressed any worse. He seemed more stable. The nurses encouraged me to go home and rest, and they would call me if anything changed.

Mom brought me back, and she and I changed into more comfortable clothing. Mom decided she couldn't just sit still, so she decided to straighten up my kitchen for me. I sat there on the recliner and told Mom that I was going to go to my prayer closet. Back in March of that year, Robert built me a little prayer closet for my birthday. I had fallen in love with the movie *War Room*, and the prayer closet in that movie inspired me to want one when Robert and I were desperate for answers for his health. I had been in that little room so many times praying and reading my Bible. Little did I know at the time, my prayers weren't getting past my ceiling.

As Mom began to clean, I went back to my closet, turned on the light, and pulled the door shut behind me. I chose to sit on the floor instead of the little chair that I had in there. I used my grandpa's Bible, which was given to me after he passed away in 2010. I used it to do my devotionals when I went in there. I grabbed that Bible off the chair and held it tightly.

I had no words to even pray. I just started crying and then spoke to God, "Robert built this prayer closet for me to get closer to You, and now how Ironic I am now using it to beg You for his life."

I sat there looking at that Bible. "God, I need to hear from You. I need guidance. I need something. Please speak to me through this Bible."

I just began to turn the pages in the book. As I did, this little Post-it note fell out onto my lap. I had never seen it before. It was my grandmother's handwriting, and it had a single verse written on it. That verse was Matthew 18:20, "For where two or three are gathered in my name, there am I in the midst of them."

I flipped to that chapter and read that verse. I laid my Bible down and left the prayer closet. I went to my mom and looked at her. "Mom, I think God wants us to pray. Will you pray with me? He said where two or three are gathered in His name, so will you pray with me?"

My mom happily obliged, and we knelt on our knees in front of the couch, and we prayed. After we prayed, I received another phone call from the hospital. He had taken a turn for the worse.

It was approaching daylight, so I went on and showered and went back up there. On my way there, that Bible verse kept repeating in my mind, "For where two or three are gathered in my name, there am I in the midst of them," so I thought, *I need to get more people praying.*

I was able to call a few preachers and had them praying, and then my sister was able to get in touch with the wife of a pastor whom I bonded with years ago when I was only a teenager. This pastor prayed with me and even counseled me over the phone when I came out of an abusive relationship. As years passed, I lost contact with this pastor. He had lived in Michigan. Little did I know that he now resided in North Carolina just two hours away from me. My sister was friends with his wife on Facebook. She was able to get word to him to have him call me. We spoke on the phone, and I explained what I was facing and asked him to please pray for my husband. I knew in my heart that if I wanted anyone in my corner who could get his prayers through to God, it was Pastor Jon Jenkins. I had my former pastor Darrel Cox, Evangelist Jimmy Clark, and now Pastor Jenkins all calling me daily, checking in, praying with me and over my husband.

That afternoon, a team of doctors came into Robert's room to speak to Robert's parents and me about his condition. Things were not looking good. They explained what they had been doing, that they now plan to do a series of testing to check for brain activity. They also introduced us to donor services. Robert was listed as a donor, so they came in to explain those procedures. This was not looking good, but I was not about to lose hope. I had the best of the best praying for him. I had thousands of Christians, most of whom I didn't even know, praying for him, My God is capable of healing him and turn this around. I refused to believe any differently.

That night, I went to grab dinner with my family. We were back at my home, and as we were sitting around my kitchen table, the house echoed with everyone's voices. I sat there just feeling so numb. I kept reciting that verse in my head, "Where two or three are gathered."

The sounds around me became dampened, and it seemed more like a roar of white noise. Then I remember looking up from the table at my sister and my dad, who were sitting next to me. "The prayers aren't for Robert. They are for me!" I mumbled out. The realization pierced my heart. It was as if God or one of His angels whispered that right into my soul.

At that moment, I knew Robert would never step foot back into this home with me ever again. That night I went back, my mom and my sister decided to stay the night in that hospital room with me because I refused to leave his side. I wanted so desperately to feel hopeful, that something could change and he somehow would miraculously be healed, and we could continue living out our dreams together. That night was long and hard. The doctors came in and told me that they would need to conduct another test for brain activity. They would do that tomorrow.

The next day, we prayed and looked for any sign of hope to cling to. They came in and informed us that Robert had failed the first test for signs of brain activity. The next step would be an imaging test of sorts to know for certain if there is any blood flow to his brain at all, basically to be able to legally declare him brain dead.

That day seemed like an eternity, waiting and waiting. The family at this point pretty much accepted the fact that Robert wasn't with us any longer, and we were preparing to move on and lay his body to rest. They had scheduled his imaging test early that evening, but for some reason, it kept getting pushed back. Robert's parents went on and said their goodbyes and left for home with broken hearts. My family decided they needed a much-needed break and some fresh air and went downstairs to head outside.

I was finally alone with Robert for the very first time since I last saw him and spoke to him at home. Everything was hitting me hard. I was alone, so I felt more comfortable breaking down within the privacy of this cold, bitter hospital room. I was sitting next to Robert, holding his lifeless hand. I couldn't even find any words. I just got up and placed myself on his bed next to him. The only problem was that it was a small hospital bed. He was a strong large man, so I was half on him and half off the bed.

The nurses were able to see via the cameras what I was doing and, without hesitation, came in. "Mrs. Wall, don't move. We want to help you be more comfortable." All three grabbed the sheeting on his right side of the bed and moved him farther over to that side, allowing me a little more room to lie with him. They exited the room, and I wrapped my arm through his and laid my head on his chest.

I lost it. I lay there bawling, wailing, and mourning him. How in the world could this be? We just got married. It hasn't even been two years yet. He had been my best friend for seven years. This wasn't fair.

My tears were running down his chest. I held on tightly to him, asking him how he could leave me like this. This wasn't the plan. This wasn't fair. I was angry and broken. He promised me that he would never leave me. "What now? What now, Robert? What am I supposed to do now?" I was so broken. "We were just getting started, and now I am left here without you." I cried and I cried. I just kept asking God how I was supposed to make it through this.

As my tears began to soften, I opened my eyes. They were immediately directed to the footboard of Robert's bed. All I could see was this large number five. As soon as I looked at that five, God reminded me immediately of that moment in the car with the five red roses. "Five is the number of grace." That is how I was going to make it through it, by God's grace.

The medical team came in and informed me that they would be preparing Robert to go down for his testing. My mom and sister had now arrived back in the room, and they sat there and waited for the results with me.

Within an hour or so, Robert was being wheeled back into his room. The nurses were buzzing around him, trying to get all his equipment hooked back up properly. They informed me that the doctor would be up shortly to discuss the results with me. I, my mother, and my sister sat there waiting. We were prepared for the news that he would be medically claimed deceased. We had gospel music playing to ease the sadness in the room.

The song playing was "Didn't I Walk on the Water" by the Dunaway family.

> As I kneel in the darkness in the middle of the night, I'm praying for assurance everything's going to be all right. And, Lord, I see another battle, and it's right in front of me. I'm afraid I won't be able, and I'll go down in defeat. And He said, "Do you remember where I brought you from? Just take another look behind you at how far you've come." Oh, and every time you ask Me, didn't I deliver you? So why would you be thinking that I wouldn't see you through? Didn't I walk on the water and calm the raging sea. I spoke to the wind. It hushed, and I gave you peace. Didn't I run to your rescue? Didn't I hear you when you called? I walked right beside you just so you wouldn't fall. Didn't I leave all of heaven just to die for your sins? I searched until I found you, and I'd do it all again."

Listening to those lyrics, God reminded me that He is sovereign. Though we were praying for healing, God chose the ultimate healing and took Him home. God reached out in my darkest hour, and He delivered me. He left all of heaven to die for my sin, and He saved me. He didn't just answer the prayers of healing Robert, He saved me so that I can one day see him again. Oh, my goodness. The mercy that His love had shown around me.

The doctor and staff entered the room. "Mrs. Wall, unfortunately, we cannot declare your husband legally brain dead. There is still a small amount of blood flow reaching the farthest back part of his brain. It is highly unlikely that he will ever recover from this with any quality of life. You have two options: you may leave the decision up to the donor services of when to remove his life support to harvest his organs, or you may work with the hospital staff to have your husband moved to a long-care nursing facility, where he will be kept on life support with a feeding tube until that last part of his brain no longer receives blood flow."

I heard Karen Peck singing in the back ground "Four Days Late." That song started giving me peace that God is here, and I looked over at him, and my poor mother, still clinging on to that little bit of hope, looked at me with wide eyes in hopeful desperation God can still fix this. However, looking at Robert lying in that bed hooked up to machines, that is not a life he would ever want to live. He has said to me time and time again to never let him live like that. The decision was easy because Robert had already made it for me. He wasn't in that shell of a body any longer anyway. God allowed us this week to prepare our hearts for his passing and to be able to say our goodbyes and to touch him and love him while his body was still being kept warm by the machines.

I told the doctor that he was not going to a facility to live on machines just for my sake, that I wanted him to be able to keep his dignity and be allowed to pass away the way he would want. I was then greeted by the donor services and was assisted in preparing the documents for the release of his body to their care.

That night, I went home in a million pieces, but this time, unlike the first night he entered the hospital, I had peace and assurance I was going to see him again. I didn't go home alone, I now had God. I may be getting ready to bury my husband, but God was carrying me and was pouring so much grace over me already in such a short time.

CHAPTER 8

Finding Strength

On November 14, 2020, we said our final goodbyes as we laid our sweet Robert to rest. I believe in my entire heart that Robert was never with us during his stay in the hospital. I have felt time and time again that he truly went home to be with the Lord on November 7, 2020. During our week in the hospital, he was hooked up to machines that were keeping his organs vital and operating, but his soul didn't remain. God gave his parents and me that week to grasp what was happening to allow us some type of closure in saying our final goodbyes. Those lasting days are mostly a blur for me, but there were times that I do recall seeing God with me in the hours I was at my weakest and most vulnerable.

I called upon God to save me on November 8, but it still hadn't registered to me that I had just become a child of God. My grief was so heavy and overshadowed any logic or reasoning that I could obtain for myself. I felt like I was in the deepest and darkest hole that I had ever found myself in. My sweet mother lived with me for two solid weeks until she had to force herself to go back to her life and work. She wanted to just stay and be with me all hours of the day, but life keeps moving even when we feel our world has just stopped.

During the days, I was able to keep moving and keep myself busy, but the moment the sun set and I found myself utterly and completely alone in the home that Robert and I were just beginning to build our life in, I struggled. I became eaten up with fear and desolation. Months before Robert's death, I had been battling extreme anxiety and other health issues myself. One of my physicians put me on a combination of medications, one of which has a horrible reaction to 390 other medications prescribed and over the counter. This medication also reacted horribly to my grief. I found myself three separate times in the ER with signs of a heart attack. Thankfully God was with me, and He protected me every time.

I was weaned off these medications to prevent any further complications, but I found myself now suffering from PTSD from finding Robert dead in his car to now also PTSD from the trauma this medication had put me through. I experienced God in a great and mighty way.

I also experienced Satan in a very real and powerful way. The night before the funeral, I was starting to feel extremely run-down and sick with congestion. I was also experiencing extreme heartburn. Without any thought, I grabbed my bottle of Pepcid and began to chew them, then the thought hit me. I can't take this with this other medication in my system.

I immediately ran to the kitchen sink and spit it all out and gargled with water. Panic began to set in. See, the devil had already begun to work in my mind that I was next. He told me every night and every morning that I was his and that I was next to die. My children will be left without their mother. Don't worry. They will be taken care of. I had a very nice life insurance policy in place that would guarantee them a better future for them than I could ever give them alive.

As I was pacing the floor in a state of panic, I kept praying, "God, I am scared. I don't want to die. God, my children need me. I can't function. I can't breathe. I can't even help myself get rid of this simple heartburn."

My poor mother was standing in the kitchen, watching as her child is stricken with so much grief, fear, and pain, and I know she was feeling helpless. She just stood there, quietly praying to God and interceding for me. It was all she knew she could do.

My anxiety began to grow stronger the harder I tried to soothe myself. I kept pacing, and I found myself pacing back toward my bedroom, the room I haven't been able to allow myself to go into since Robert passed away. I went in only to quickly shower and grab clothing, but I could never sleep in there. But this night, I found myself walking in with tears streaming down my face and engulfed in so much fear and panic. I fell to Robert's side of the bed, my knees hitting the floor, tears soaking up the bedsheets, just begging God for His Help. "God, I need You. I can't do this. I can't do this without You. I am not supposed to be here. God, we had so many dreams and aspirations, and now they are all gone. I can't even help myself get rid of this heartburn or congestion. I can't take even the slightest little thing to help relieve the symptoms that make me feel the taunts of me dying are real. God, I need You to help me. I need You so much."

I picked myself up and walked back into the living room, where I found my mother on the couch sitting, worried for me. I cuddled up beside her and laid my head on her shoulder and just tried to breathe the best I could. I sat there for only a couple of minutes, and I noticed God. God took hold of me. He took away every bit of my sinus congestion and my heartburn. It immediately vanished.

I lifted my head in amazement and looked at my mom, and she looked at me and smiled. I didn't even say anything to her yet. She looked at me and said, "It's all gone, isn't it?"

I grasped to find the words. I was just astonished. "*Yes*, it's all gone, the heartburn the congestion. I can breathe. There's no more mucus in my throat. Momma, God just took it from me!"

She grabbed my hand and held it tightly and said, "God promised to take care of you, and He is showing Himself faithful. It's going to be okay."

God allowed me to see Him the night He opened my eyes to how lost I truly was. Now He has shown Himself to me once again. So many people know God and experience His love and blessings in their lives as Christians, but it's truly a blessing when God allows one of His children to see Him, not just hear Him or witness the blessings He bestows upon them, but to *see* Him.

When you see God in your life, it changes you. It changes everything about you—how you think and how you react to things. Through this journey, God revealed Himself to me several times.

Days following the burial of Robert, I tried my best every day to wake up, get dressed, move, and fill my mind with other things just in hopes to keep me viable for my children. I decided that maybe if I went back to work, I would find a sense of purpose. I called the owner of the salon that I managed and informed him that I would be back at work the following Monday. He encouraged me that there was no hurry for me to come back, considering what I was facing and that he had things under control, but he also realized that maybe work would be a welcome distraction for me as well and agreed to see me back on Monday.

Monday morning, I woke up and cried for two solid hours. I hadn't slept well because the nights suffocate me with fear, and my thoughts torment me. I managed to get through the tears, and I drove to work. Once I got there, I was greeted with love from my staff, welcoming me back. I drove straight in and went to work. On the first day, I got through. The second day, I arrived and met with the owner. He instructed me that he had set up a couple of interviews for a new stylist. He asked if I wanted to take over and complete the interviews myself, or would I rather he still go on and conduct them himself. I chose to go ahead and take on my role as manager and complete the task at hand.

The interviews weren't scheduled till the following day, so I had time to prepare and look over all my salon owner's notes so I could be responsible for the search for qualifying candidates for the roles to be filled. The next morning, I had two interviews back-to-back, both of which seemed exactly what we were looking for. One of the ladies came from another salon that I had a great experience in, and she had worked for that company for many years as a salon manager herself. She had moved away to another state and recently moved back to take care of a sick parent and was searching for employment.

I remember as I was interviewing her, all I could think of was she would be a great asset to me and the team, but I also kept fighting my grief. It took everything in me to hide my grief and to be professional. Once the interviews were completed, I went back out on the floor and began to receive clients, and I found myself struggling. You see, the salon I worked at was in the territory my husband had worked. He would stop by almost every single day to just stop in to see me and sometimes brought goodies for my girls to enjoy on their breaks. I couldn't look out the front window without seeing trucks pass through that looked exactly like his work truck.

Panic of my reality began to set in. None of these trucks were his, and he was not going to be walking through those doors to greet us anymore. The entire rest of that morning, I kept having to excuse myself from clients to go to the bathroom to cry and try to keep my face from showing the pain I was feeling. I finally got to a point I told God I couldn't do this. I didn't know how to do this. Here I was the manager of this great salon with a team of ladies who depended on my leadership, and I couldn't even lead myself. I was hiding in the bathroom, falling apart.

I stepped back out onto the salon floor and mustered up the strength and courage to finish the service of the client who was patiently waiting on me to get my act together. After I was able to finish up, I quietly cleaned up my station, packed up all my things, and told my team that I couldn't finish the day. I had to go home. They all understood, and I left my senior stylist in charge.

All the way home I couldn't breathe. I had messaged the owner to inform him that I was headed home for the rest of the day and why. He told me he understood and to call him later to discuss the interviews that I had earlier that morning. On my fifty-minute drive home, I talked to God about how I felt so defeated, that it was harder on me being there at work than it was at home. So many memories of Robert coming by and adorning me there, it was killing me. I didn't know how I could go back, yet I needed my job. I couldn't just quit. I had children to provide for. I now had a mountain of bills all left to my sole income to pay. How was I going to do this? God, I don't know what to do.

I tried to call my health coach and friend Erica. I was aiming to get some advice and to see if I could somehow manage to increase my income with my health coaching business that I just started on the side that summer. I called a few times but no answer. I gave up, and on the last bit of the drive home, I just tried to silence my mind.

As my mind became silent, I heard the smallest voice tell me, "Have faith in me, child. I will take care of you. Stop looking for advice from others and just trust Me."

What? Where was that coming from? God, I do trust You, but I am scared to death of my future.

By the time I got home, I was sobbing in tears. I tried to call my parents, but they didn't answer either. I knew I had to call my boss, and I didn't know what I was going to tell him. I didn't want to mess up or make the wrong decision. So much was now dependent on me, so I thought. I was starting to feel desperate for answers, but no one was available for me to speak to.

Little did I know, God was blocking me from reaching out to others. In my desperation, I have found myself always turning to my Bible. It was my Bible at all hours of the day that I would reach for and turn to when I began to feel scared, overwhelmed, lonely, or like I was dying. So at this moment, this was no different. I plopped down in my recliner and grabbed my Bible, telling God I needed Him to speak to me, and I opened my Bible and just read where it fell open, which was Isaiah 41:10: "Fear thou not; for I am with thee: be not dismayed; for I am thy God: I will strengthen thee; yea, I will help thee; yea, I will uphold thee with the right hand of my righteousness."

I sat there soaking in that verse. I flipped through my Bible, and I saw another piece of scripture stating not to look to others but to trust God. I sat there in tears of shame. I told God I was sorry that I wasn't trusting Him fully and felt that I needed guidance from others before just making this move.

My phone rang, and it was my parents. My mother could tell that I was crying and was upset, and she kept urging me to tell her what I was battling at that moment. I began to tell her my concerns and fears but how I also felt God was trying to tell me to take a step in faith and trust Him. I no more got the words out of my mouth and my dad spoke up in the background. He immediately just said, "Quit."

What? Did I just hear him correctly? I can't just quit—

"Trisha, quit your job. Yes, it's scary, but God will provide for you. Quit your job."

My parents told me to pray and give it to God and then call my boss. I hung up the phone, and as soon as our call ended, the phone was ringing. It was my boss. My heart began to race. I just got off the phone with my parents. I haven't had time to pray over this, but God said to take the call. I answered the call and began to speak to my boss. Then out of nowhere, as I was updating him on the interviews, God whispered in my ears, "I know you worry over this salon being taken care of. I have taken care of that for you. You interviewed your replacement this morning. Tell him about her and the role you feel she is best suited for and that your role as manager and let him know you will not be returning."

I could hear the voice of my boss speaking, but my mind was focused on the voice I had just heard. I took a deep breath and informed my boss of how I was struggling, but I explained how the lady I interviewed this morning I felt would make a great replacement for me, and the other would make a great placement for the role that we needed to fill. He so kindly explained to me that he understood and that there was no rule book for how to experience life after suddenly losing your spouse to death, that he couldn't even imagine what I was going through, that it just made him cherish his moments with his wife and children that much more. He told me not to worry about the salon, that it would be fine and that I would have an open door there if I ever wanted to come back.

I concluded that call with a much grateful thank-you and hung up. I sat there for a while, just trying to grasp the magnitude of that burden being lifted off my shoulders. I was not alone. God was holding me and telling me it was going to be okay. God provided for me in every way and has every day since. I took much-needed time to grieve and grow.

CHAPTER 9

The Guidance of God

Thanksgiving and Christmas have now passed me by. The holidays of this particular year were calmer, more solemn, and full of tears than years past. I can't even recall most of anything that happened. I just know I was surrounded by my family, and their love and strength helped carry me through the day.

Robert left me with one last gift of his love. He had booked and paid for a second-anniversary trip to Maui. He fell in love with the island on our honeymoon the year prior and just couldn't wait to go back. After his passing, only his portion of the trip was refundable, so my family and grief counselor encouraged me to still go and take someone with me. I chose to take my sister. My sister and I, as I stated earlier on in this book, have always had a tight bond and friendship. Robert always encouraged me to take trips and spend time with her more often than we ever did. I knew there was no one better to ask that would make Robert happy to know to go with me than Jennifer.

The trip was set for our second wedding anniversary, which was quickly approaching: January 7, 2021. It was a trip set for eight days. The flight, the accommodations, the rental car—everything was already taken care of. Robert had it planned to a dime. My heart was heavy, and I felt it was going to be so bittersweet going back to where he and I spent our honeymoon but this time knowing he was no longer with me. That was hard to swallow, but I went. My therapist thought the time away would be a helpful part of my healing process.

The flight there was calm and mellow. We slept most of the way. Once the plane arrived on the island, the joy and excitement flooded my heart. Maui has always carried my heart, and once my feet hit the soil I felt at home. If you have never been to the Hawaiian Islands, I must tell you, there is just something in and of itself that is healing on those islands. I don't know if it is the warm salty sea air or the loving, laid-back nature of the people or what, but it was good for me indeed.

Once we arrived, we went straight to the car rental to pick up our ride. Robert had asked for a convertible sports car. When we were ushered down to where the car was to be picked up, we were greeted by the guy asking us if we would consider trading out the sports car for a utility vehicle. At that moment, I was tired and didn't care. I just wanted to get to my hotel room, so I agreed. I have always wanted a jeep since I was a teenager, and my dad wouldn't let me have one because he rolled his when he was younger. So to my happy surprise, he led us to a row of Jeep Wranglers and said, "You can have your pick."

I couldn't help but laugh inside and told God that He was amazing and that I loved Him. I picked the beautiful teal-green one because it was my favorite color. Jennifer laughed and stated that she knew I was going to choose that one. Full of excitement once more, we loaded her up and hit the road to find our beautiful ocean-side hotel.

We had a little bit of a drive to get there, but the winding roads along the edge of the island gave us some of the prettiest views. It was truly paradise. Once we arrived at the hotel and I was checking in, the lady at the desk wished me a happy anniversary and then asked where Mr. Wall was. My heart broke into a million pieces once again as I had to explain the sad truth, which was now my reality. She immediately showed compassion and started typing away and said, "Mrs. Wall, it appears that you have booked an ocean-view room. If it is okay, I would like to relocate you to the garden and oceanfront view. Our prayers and hearts are with you during this difficult time. If we can help make this trip any easier for you, please let us know."

I humbly offered my gratitude, and Jennifer and I made our way up to the room. Even there at that moment, I was in awe of how God just kept pouring His love onto us. First, the jeep upgrade and now this stunning room upgrade. I could just feel His presence with me.

Every morning that week, I found myself waking up at 4:30 a.m. I never can go back to sleep, and I didn't want to disturb my sister's rest, so I would grab my Bible and step out on the Lani. It would always be so dark out there minus the lights that lit the sidewalks and all the Lanis. I would have just enough of a warm amber glow to read the scriptures. Those mornings were the most intimate times that I have ever had with God. He would meet me there every morning, and though my heart felt so worn and broken, He held me tightly and restored peace and love in my heart. Those mornings I would sometimes find my heart crying out to God in prayer, and other mornings, I would be so lost for words that I couldn't even pray. I could only muster up tears. But I knew that God counted my tears as prayers, and He knew my heart, and He felt my pain. He comforted me in ways no one ever could.

The third morning that I woke up and met Him on my Lani, I found so much comfort in my Bible reading. Every scripture that I turned to was filled with his promises to provide, comfort, and be with me daily. He promised to be my husbandman, now that I was a widow, and that He would fill my heart with love and would give me so much grace to walk this journey.

I don't know what it was about that morning, but His presence was so strong and real. I started praising His name and worshipping Him. I couldn't hold back telling Him how much I loved Him and needed Him. How thankful that I was to have His love.

The entire time that I was praising His name, the sun still hadn't come up yet, but it was getting close to sunrise. The birds seemed to have woken up, and they were singing so loudly. I pulled out my phone and videoed it because it was so amazing. It was a moment I never wanted to forget. Those birds never chirped so loudly or as early as they did that day. I knew in my heart that it wasn't a coincidence. God was there. He was all around me and in that space.

Those birds were singing and worshiping Him as well. God gave me so much peace and restoration on that island that week. He allowed me to get so close to Him, and at that moment, I felt my broken heart slowly begin to heal.

On the way home, we had a layover to connect a flight out of Colorado back to Charlotte. I chose to wear a hoodie that my doctor's wife made and sold for a short time. On the front of it, it read, "Be Salty, Mark 9:50." It is my most favorite hoodie to wear.

As Jennifer and I were waiting to board our flight, the head stewardess called me up to the podium and asked for our ticket information. She took notice of my hoodie and commented that she loved it and started asking about it. A few others came up, and she asked me to wait for a second as she took care of their assigned seating, then when she was finished, she smiled at me and said, "You know what, I have two first-class seats open. I am going to bump you and your friend up to those seats."

Oh, my goodness! God, You just keep spoiling me. He just kept showing up and showing out with His love and kindness.

Once we boarded and got settled into our seats, I quickly realized that God was looking out for me. That entire flight home, I battled a horrible panic attack that I hadn't experienced all week. He knew that if I had been in coach, I would have been a lot worse. Even in the small things God, is good.

Now we are back home, and reality is setting in once again. The fear in the night has come back upon me. The tears never seem to stop. What once was home now feels cold and indifferent. Every single night, I found myself crying and begging God to walk the halls and each room, to watch over me in my sleep, to guard and protect my mind from Satan's lies.

Satan still fought me daily. It seemed the closer I got to God, the more he would try to knock me off my feet. One night, I just couldn't bear to be in that house alone, so I called my parents and told them that I was staying the night with them. They told me to come on, that they were just watching an old movie and would love to have me. I came over there and sat there so full of anxiety.

After the movie was over, they decided they were ready for bed, and I told them I preferred to sleep on the couch instead of in the guest room, so Mom brought me a pillow and a nice warm blanket. Lights were shut off, and the house fell silent. I lay there in the dark of the home that I grew up in, and I listened to all the cricks of the house settling in the night. I talked to God till I fell asleep.

That night, I was awakened by the most grueling sight of the darkest vision of a figure. It was hovering over me, laughing at me, telling me that I was next, and I was his, and I was going to hell. I just started screaming to get away from me. "You are the devil. You are the devil. I'm God's, and you are devil."

My screams woke my parents up, and my mom came running into the living room to make sure I was okay. Once she flipped on the lights, the image disappeared. I just lay there, crying and hyperventilating yet trying to tell my mother I was okay. She kept asking me if I was sure, and I said that I was and to go back to bed. I started praying immediately, asking God for His protection. I knew that I now not only have seen God in my life, but Satan has even revealed himself to me.

Every day after that, I began to wonder, was I saved? I mean, how could I truly know? I thought for thirty-six years of my life I was saved just to find out from God Himself that I was not. Did I get saved in my living room that night on November 8, *or* am I somehow still being deceived? But no. How can I feel the love of God like I have and not be saved. It has been a thing in my mind now that I was now always looking for assurance.

I found myself in my Bible multiple times a day and night. I was talking to God every second of the day, whether it was silently in my head or aloud. Most mornings, I found myself when I was showering, singing and praising His name, then I would find myself in prayer for something very specific that I couldn't understand why I was even praying for it. I was not wanting it. I was not ready for it. I even told God while I was praying that I wasn't ready for this yet, but He knew the reasoning He has laid it on my heart to pray for it, and perhaps it was for later in my future. But every day, this prayer became much stronger. It took more time to ask for, and it became very specific.

I do feel that sometimes, God lays things on your heart and instills in you what to pray so that He may intercede for you in those prayers, and I believe this is what He was doing for me. I promised my life to God, and I told God that I was His and that I am ashamed for wasting my entire life living for myself, that if He would allow me, I wanted to make up for all that time wasted and serve Him in whichever way He could use me for His glory.

The first Sunday after we had lain Robert to rest, my parents decided to attend their former church, Woodland Baptist Church, and I went along with them. Robert and I joined my dad's church after we got married, and since my dad wouldn't be preaching there due to the funeral the day before, I went along with them. I remember when I walked into that church as I approached the doors leading into the auditorium, that still small voice whispered in my ear once more, "This is your home."

I shook my head like, *What? No, my home church is with my parents at Lighthouse. I need to be with my parents right now.*

I remember being greeted with so much love and compassion from people whom knew me, but I didn't know them. I sat in that service just feeling so numb, and then Pastor Gammons had the altar call. My daddy grabbed me by the hand, and he and my mom escorted me to that altar, where they both laid their hands on me and prayed over me.

After church, the car ride was quiet. I remember sitting in the back seat just gazing out the window and thinking to myself, *"This is your home?" God, I don't even know why You would say that to me. You know I need my parents more than I ever have right now.*

I no more got that thought out than my mom turned around in her seat so that she could see me and said, "Tricia, while your dad and I prayed over you this morning at the altar, we felt that God wants you and your children to move your membership back to Woodland. We know you probably want to stay with us, but, honey, we think God has your future there in that church in some form, whether it's a ministry He can use you in, or maybe it's even a future man of God to marry. We just think that is where God wants you right now."

I couldn't even pick my jaw up off the floorboard of the car. I was flabbergasted. There is no way they could hear what I heard when I walked into that church. There is no way they heard my thoughts just now, telling God I needed to be at Lighthouse and not Woodland.

I spoke up and told them both what I had heard and that I was back here struggling with it because I felt I needed to be with them. Daddy assured me that he wanted me to stay with them as well and that I will always be welcome there, but he agreed that he felt God was trying to guide me where He wanted me, and that was Woodland Baptist Church. He assured me that I wouldn't be alone and reminded me that my brother and his wife, Lauren, were there, and I could stay with them.

I didn't fight it. I followed that call and went back to Woodland. I wasn't sure what God was up to, but I knew He had me in prayers upon prayers for something specific, and now He is moving me back to Woodland. All I knew is that I was just trying every day to serve Him and be obedient and allow Him to carry me through my grief.

CHAPTER 10

God's Grace

Facing grief is something that no two people will ever face the same way. I have learned on this journey I most certainly never expected to see myself on that there are two kinds of people: the people who love you with sincere love and support you who just try to lift you up in your darkest hour, and then there are those people who will judge every move you make and question you. Satan used this to try to tear me down when I felt I couldn't be brought any lower. He continued to step in and kick me when I was down.

I found myself struggling to face the days ahead of me. I had two children who depended on me, and I fought my struggles to get up, get dressed, and keep moving forward even if it was just baby steps. I knew despite what I was going through, I deserved happiness. Robert loved me, and he lived his life in a way that he always put my happiness first. When I was happy, he was happy. I reminded myself of that every single day. Robert would have wanted me to get up and try to find some joy in the days ahead. I knew that even more, God wanted to restore my joy.

Every time someone would show up and show themselves ugly toward me, God reminded me that it was just a tool of Satan trying to keep me broken, but God had greater plans, and I was to trust Him and just stay faithful in His Word. He promised in John 15:7, 11, "If ye abide in me, and my words abide in you, ye shall ask what we will, and it shall be done unto you. These things have I spoken unto you, that My *joy* might remain in you, and that *your joy* might be full."

I found myself just looking to keep busy and find joy. Thankfully, my sister-in-law Lauren was a stay-at-home mother of my favorite little nephew, Barrett, whom I call "Opie." She welcomed me into her home every single day. I basically lived there during the days till I had to go back home in the evenings. Lauren became the person whom I could open myself up and share my fears and grief with. God used her in so many ways to help me and comfort and inspire me during those dark times. She and I grew so close together. We would go eat breakfast every morning, hang out in the yard with Opie, or sometimes we would get a wild hair and find ourselves going hiking somewhere. She kept me busy. She was there to share God's Word with me as well as to pray with me over the things in my life that I needed support for.

Lauren has always been blunt in everything she says and does, and I remember in December of 2020, she came to me. "Trish, there is someone at church that I think you need to meet."

I looked at her like she was an idiot and told her, "No, thank you. I had just buried my husband just a month ago," and we dropped it.

February was here, and she brought it up again. This time, I looked at her and didn't even speak. She looked at me and asked what I thought. "Lauren, to be honest, I am not sure what I think. Can I tell you something that I haven't shared with anyone?"

She responded that of course, I could trust her to share.

"Lauren, for the past two months, I have been praying for something that I know my heart has not been ready to pray for. I haven't understood why I am even praying for it, but I know my prayers are growing to be very specific in nature. I don't know how to admit this, but I have been praying that God will not allow me to die alone, that He will restore love back into my life, someone that is saved and loves God, who is serving God faithfully and will accept my story and my children, who will understand my love for Robert and will love me for all that I am, that he will love God more than he could ever love me 'cause then, I know he would love me properly."

I told her that I wasn't sure to even know how to know my heart would be ready, but I felt that God was preparing me to become ready. She said that she would be in much prayer over this with me and that I will know when God reveals it to me.

The following Sunday, she pointed out this man to me on the very far side of the church. All I could tell was that he was very tall. That was it. I just shrugged my shoulders and told her I couldn't really see him, but that it didn't matter. I was at church to focus on God, not some man.

A few weeks go by, and I watched this man to even see if he was as faithful as I had been told. In doing so, it seemed he was involved with another lady in the church, and I decided that I was not going to step on anyone's toes and dismissed this idea. I needed to be focused on God, not a man anyways. Plus, at this time, it had only been three months since I buried my husband, and I wasn't ready.

March 11, 2020, which was a Wednesday, I felt all day that God wanted me to officially join the church. My children were not with me that evening, and Lauren and Perry couldn't be there that night either. I still went to the service alone, and I felt, "Well, I will just plan to join another night when the kids are here and my family is here."

As I sat in the service, my heart rate stayed elevated; my palms were sweaty. I just couldn't stand being in my own skin. I felt so pressured by the Lord that I must join that night. So during the altar call, I walked over to Brother Zach and told him that I wanted to join the church. He passed the information along to the preacher, and the preacher announced my wanting to become a member, and he informed the church of who I was, that I was Preacher Eddie's daughter, whom they have all been praying for, whose husband passed away four months prior. This gentleman whom Lauren wanted me to meet sat on the very front row and had never noticed me before now. I tried to keep my eyes from ever looking his way. I was just so nervous being in front of everyone and was ready to just get back home.

Later that week, I had some friends whisk me away to the beach at Amelia Island, and I was able to enjoy a much-needed girls' trip away. I wasn't myself like I wanted to be, but they loved me and did their best to make sure that I had fun. On that trip, one of them was encouraging me to dip my toes back into the dating pool. I told them of the mystery guy at the church my sister-in-law was wanting me to meet, but I just wasn't sure. They encouraged me to just meet new people and slowly put myself back out there, and I did.

I told God that I was just wanting a friendship, some-one who I could spend some time with when my family was filled with their own obligations and I was left alone, someone that I could share Him and church with, and if anything amounted from it, then that would be of His doing. I did promise God that this time, I was going to do things the right way and that I was not sleeping with any man out of the realms of marriage because God meant more to me, and I did not want to lose His blessings on my life.

After I got back from Amelia Island, I met a young man who seemed to share a lot in common with me. He was raised as I was raised. At one point, he even attended my former church Trinity Baptist for a few years when I was still a member there, and somehow, he knew my entire family, but we didn't know each other. It seemed this was something worth exploring. We had our first date at a local barbecue place and then followed it up with a night of bowling. We connected so easily and just had so much fun together. I enjoyed his company and the spark we seemed to have.

After a month of seeing this guy and talking practically every day and night, he started to become a little shady and distant. He was acting weird, and I couldn't understand it at all, except for the fact I refused to sleep with him, but he always seemed so respectful of that and acted as if he agreed on that issue as well. My brother and Lauren wanted to meet him, so I asked him if he wanted to join us for bowling one night, and he said that he would love to, but then he was a no-show. I went home embarrassed and confused. His excuses were poor and made no sense.

The next day, Lauren and I decided to take advantage of the beautiful day, so we drove out to the falls on Stone Mountain. The entire day, I was just trying to analyze why he was acting the way he was. What had I done wrong? Lauren was knee-deep in this with me, trying to make sense of it all.

We found ourselves at the bottom of the mountain, and Opie wanted to play in the water, so we sat there and let him splash around in the ice-cold water. I don't know how he didn't freeze to death, but he was in absolute heaven. After about an hour, Lauren decided we needed to head back up and try to find another fall that she wanted to show me.

As we trenched back up the hundreds of stairs that led us back up the top of the mountain, Opie was getting tired and frustrated. He didn't want to leave the watering hole. He was having fun. Now he was having to walk up all these stairs, and it wasn't fun anymore. His mom kept calling him and encouraging him to just keep moving, but he kept wanting to turn around and go back to the fun watering hole. She picked him up as he was screaming and crying because he couldn't understand why we left the water. She told him, "Son, we are going to go see a much better, a much prettier and much bigger waterfall."

As I walked ahead of them and kept patiently waiting as she kept trying to get Opie to trust her, God once again spoke to me. "That's you. You keep wondering why this man is being flakey. You can't understand why I am moving him out of your life. You can't see that he isn't going to be what I need him to be in your life. I have a bigger, prettier, and better waterfall to take you to if only you will trust Me and let Me take you there."

I felt so much in awe. Once Lauren approached me, I had to immediately share with her what God had just shown me as painting her and her son as a metaphor for God and me. I just need to trust Him and where He was taking me.

I let go of this man. I stopped trying to figure out what was wrong with him, and I stopped caring. I turned my focus back on God and just stayed in my Bible, being faithful to church, and being obedient to whatever God asked of me.

Lauren later brought up this man at church again. I told her I wasn't interested in him. She began to share his story and his testimony with me, and I did find respect and some admiration toward him that God was able to change him and use him in the ways that he has, but I wasn't interested.

Somehow, that interest began to grow. I found myself looking his way and just trying to picture where he came from to where he is now, and in doing so, I began to find an attraction toward him. But every time I saw him, he seemed to be with someone else. I knew in my heart that I was never going to place myself where I didn't belong.

I later found myself praying for this man by name, and I didn't even know why. I just felt in my heart that God had big plans for this man, and he must need prayers, so I prayed for him daily. I learned that you can't invest your time praying for someone and not start to care for the people you pray for. I didn't even know this man, but I cared for him and the purpose God must have had for him a great deal.

I later told Lauren about this. I told her how I felt strongly about not wanting to disrespect any other lady if he was dating someone else. Lauren decided to go to one of her friends whose husband was friends with this gentleman and asked her to find out if he was dating anyone or would be interested in meeting someone. She had her husband approach this gentleman after church one day and found out that he was not dating anyone. He asked if he would be open to meeting me. However, he felt at the time it was too soon because I was newly widowed, and it was dropped.

I continued praying for him. I told God that I didn't know what His plans were, but there was an interest in this man that if it wasn't meant to be there, please take it away. That interest never left me. Now every time I was in church, I was catching this man staring at me. If he wasn't interested in me, then why does he keep looking at me?

Lauren never gave up. She kept encouraging me to just shake his hand or say hello, but I was so uncomfortable with that. I told her that I didn't want to be the one who breaks the ice, and I wasn't going to be the aggressive one this time. She laughed at me and said, "Well, someone needs to speak." She hounded me every church service to go say hello to this man, and at every service, I would chicken out.

One service, he was walking out of the auditorium, and I was walking back in to give my brother a dress to hand over to Lauren. As I walked past him to enter the auditorium, my eyes glanced his way, and he looked at me so intently as if to say, "I see you." I walked into that auditorium with a heart rush. *Okay, something is happening. God, what am I to do?*

I went home that night, and I prayed and prayed over him and asked for guidance. At the next church service, I told Lauren I would go say hello. When I came down from the choir, he was not at his seat, so I was not able to shake his hand and say hello on my way back to my seat, which would have been the easiest and most casual way to do so without it not looking so aggressive.

After the service, Lauren kept nudging me to just walk over to him, and I kept refusing. My brother jokingly laughed and said, "Just use brick notes."

"'Brick notes'?" I asked.

"You know, like Ernest on the *Andy Griffith Show*."

I laughed, but I thought to myself, *Might not be such a bad idea. I could write him a note minus the brick.*

The next morning after I arrived at Lauren's, I told her of the thought I had of writing a note. She loved it and was like, "Let's write it now." She told me they had a Sunday school picnic coming up, and I should invite him to that. Great idea. I found a great scripture card. I invited him to the outing, left my number inside, and dowsed it with my perfume. I went old-school on this.

The following Sunday, I planned to give it to him. He seemed to be in such a hurry to get out of the church building after the Sunday morning service. I planned to just wait, but Lauren wasn't having it. She snapped her fingers at me and told me to go after him. My goodness, this is so far out of my comfort zone.

I caught up with him and tapped him on the back of his arm. "Hi, Jacob, I wanted to give this to you. I hope you have a great day."

He surprised me with a harsh bark back "Hey, what is this?"

"It's a card."

"Yeah, but what is it?" he asked as he kept looking the envelope over.

I hadn't planned to invite you verbally, fellow, but my goodness okay. "It's an invitation to a Sunday school outing. I personally wanted to invite you."

He came off so rude. I was now embarrassed and a little bit furious inside. He responded that he believed he was on call that weekend, but he would let me know, and we parted ways. All the way back to the other side of the church, I felt so stupid, and I told my brother I knew I shouldn't have approached this man. It is not my place; he was so rude to me.

Perry seemed shocked, as did Lauren. Perry explained that he was probably nervous and felt pressure and didn't know how to respond. At this point, I didn't care. He didn't have to bark at me as he did. I was so embarrassed and mad.

Three days later, I received a text that came up as "maybe Jacob." I opened it, and lo and behold, it was Jacob from church, the man who made me feel so incredibly stupid. He was apologizing because he felt that he may have come off rudely. I laughed out loud and said, "Um, you think? Yeah, you were rude."

But as I kept reading, he explained that he indeed was taken aback by me and was nervous and didn't know what to say or what I was giving him. He told me, "Thank you for the sweet card," that he, unfortunately, wasn't going to make it to the outing, but he would like to take me to dinner sometime soon and get to know me.

After that sweet, sincere apology, I couldn't turn him down.

We had our first date on May 15, 2021. If I may draw your attention to this little detail that God revealed to me later, our first date was on the fifth month, on the fifteenth, with the year being 2021, which all numbers making up the year added up to the number five. The fifteenth is five three times over, and in total, that is five fives. Remember my telling you earlier in this book that five is the number of grace? Well, grace is pouring here.

As our conversation began to flow and the number of dates began to accumulate, we both felt in our hearts this was not by chance and that God was all in our being together. Jacob and I share so many similarities, and most importantly, we share a strong love and desire for our Lord and His will in our lives. We both bathed our relationship in prayer daily and sought out God's blessings on us. Neither of us could comprehend how quickly our emotions were beginning to evolve for one another.

One day, I shared my testimony with Jacob, and I told him how I haven't told anyone of this, but I felt I got saved the night Robert was in the hospital. I told him my life story and how I was raised and how I thought my entire life that I was saved, then that night, God showed me that I wasn't. I told him of the nightmares that I have and the way Satan comes at me, which makes me wonder if I got saved or not, but I know that I have seen God, that I hear Him speak to me. I can see Him moving in my life. But how could I know for certain that I received Christ in my life for the first time on November 8?

"Sounds like to me, honey, that you did get saved."

I told him, "I have such a love for Christ that I have never experienced before, that I find myself feeling like a lovesick puppy towards God. He is all I think about. I talk to him all day long. I can't stop telling Him how much I love Him and appreciate Him. He is the last thing on my mind at night and the first thing on my mind of the morning, that even in this new relationship, that love for God trumps what I feel towards you."

Jacob smiled so excitedly and said, "You received Christ. You got the goods, babe."

The next morning at church, God allowed me the assurance that I was looking for. The preacher got up and preached on the signs of a new convert. I sat there, and everything he said about that new Christian's experience, I was checking off in my head. I am a new Christian. I am learning that everything I thought I knew about God and the Bible from growing up, under it all, I knew nothing at all. I am now seeing things so differently. I now can understand my Bible clearly when I read it, and I now experience conviction in my life of things that never used to bother me.

I no longer can allow myself to watch certain things on TV or listen to certain music on the radio. I now feel immediate shame if my mouth slips up and out comes a word that used to be used habitually before I was saved. I can't find comfort in talking about other people or judging them in any way. God will not allow me to carry malice in my heart or grudging feeling toward anyone.

He is teaching me to love as He loves, to show compassion, and to be a light unto others so that they may see Christ in me. He has given me a burden for lost souls, specifically for those who are deceived by religion and think they are going to heaven because they are good people or because they repeated prayer or were raised in a Christian home.

I was a good person. I helped people. I tried to live a good life, but I was on my way to hell. I thought I knew God because I grew up in church because I repeated the Sinner's prayer with my head and not with my heart. I was going to hell by the way of a church pew. It burdens me with how many *Christians* are in our churches whom Satan has deceived so deeply to believe they are saved when, in fact, they are nothing more than religious.

Jesus wills that no man should perish and go to hell. He said *believe in your heart,* call upon His name, and you shall be saved. Looking back over my life as I have so vulnerably shared with you in this book, I can see how God was reaching for me and calling me to Him for so long, but Satan had me completely blinded. God had to break me into a million pieces to reach me. It was His purpose to reach me, rescue me, and restore me.

God loves you, and He wants to give you life eternal. I don't deserve Him. You don't deserve Him, but He loves even us, and He died to set us free. Don't let Satan blind you into thinking you are saved from an eternity in hell when you may not be.

You know, the entire thirty-six years that I thought I was saved, I never once doubted my salvation, and the irony now that I know I am saved, Satan comes at me constantly, trying to tell me I am not saved, and I am going to hell. When you aren't saved, *he* does not need to convince you that you are. He is happy to keep lying to you, telling you that you are to keep you from becoming saved.

God found me in my brokenness. He saved me from myself. He is carrying me in my journey of grief, a journey I know for a fact I wouldn't make it through every single day if I wasn't now saved and had the grace of God pouring over me. I am nothing, but I am His. He can restore your joy. He can take what once was broken and mend it back into something so beautiful. *A life without* Christ isn't a life at all.

I never expected to lose my husband to death, but God stepped in and rescued me and gave me a gift that I will now one day be reunited with him in heaven. He also moved every piece in His time to restore all that was lost. Jacob and I married only after five months of dating. We married on October 23, 2021. On our honeymoon, we laughed in amazement at the number five that has been consistent in our relationship. God brought Jake into my life only five months after burying my sweet Robert. He had me praying every day for my future spouse for five months even when my heart wasn't looking for that. Our wedding date consists of a total of four fives. God has opened every door, and He has been at the center of every move that I make. He comes first in my life, and because of Him, I have joy renewed.

I am married, and I am happy, but that doesn't mean my grief is over. I still battle strong bits of grief. Some days are great, and other days, I can barely make it through the day. Some can look at my getting remarried as a notion of moving on or moving on too soon, but I see it as a blessing that God saw I needed someone to walk with me through this grief, to be here with me on the nights I can't breathe, and when panic and anxiety overrun me. He has given me someone who is grounded in the Word of God, who in turn helps keep me grounded when Satan attacks me.

My grief is not gone just because I have found love once again. My memories of Robert have not been buried, and my love for him has not died. I have been blessed with a love today who understands this and allows me to feel what I feel, and he comforts me when the pain is too great to bear. God has always stepped ahead of me on this journey. He has known every need before I have known my need, and He has supplied me with what I need to make it through. His grace has been sufficient, and His love is more than enough.

Grief is hard for anyone, and I feel it's even harder for those who do not know the Lord. I struggled; I still struggle. What I find that helps me more than anything is when those moments hit me hard, my breath is taken, and my chest is constricted, I close my eyes, I sit still, I take deep breaths, and instead of focusing on my loss and the pain that I feel, I begin to tell God how amazing that He is. I tell God how much I love Him. I tell God how thankful I am for His allowing me the seven years of knowing Robert and having him in my life. I thank Him for His love and His promise to be my comforter in my time of need. I thank Him for my salvation that now gives me the promise to see Robert again. I worship Him and His sovereignty.

When you feel all hope is lost, stop, take in all the blessings He has given you, and worship God. In praising Him, you will find peace and joy that you simply cannot explain. It's because of this I am finding great healing in a situation that seemed like I would never recover from.

If you do not know Christ as your personal Savior, please accept Him today before it's too late. We are never promised a tomorrow. Robert and I woke up like any other morning. We never imagined that day would be his last. Thankfully, *he* knew Christ as his Savior. Do you?

Being religious, being a good person—those are all great, but they will not get you to heaven. You must see yourself as the sinner that you are and realize that you cannot save yourself. It is only by the blood of Christ that can wash away the sin debt that will set you free and give you life eternal. You must believe in your heart that Jesus died on the cross to save you from your sin, repent of all your sins, and accept Him into your heart to be saved.

> For all have sinned and come short of the glory of God. (Romans 3:23)

> As it is written, there is None righteous, no not one. (Romans 3:10)

> For the wages of sin is death; but the gift of God is eternal life through Jesus Christ our Lord. (Romans 6:23)

> Not by Works of Righteousness that we have done, but according to his mercy he saved us, by the washing of regeneration, and renewing of the Holy Ghost; Which He shed on us abundantly through Jesus Christ our Saviour; That being justified by His grace, we should be made heirs according to the hope of eternal life. (Titus 3:5–7)

Who hath saved us...not according to our works, but according to his purpose and grace. (2 Timothy 1:9)

For there is one God and one mediator between God and men, the man Christ Jesus: Who gave himself a ransom for all, to be testified in due time. (1 Timothy 2:5, 6)

For whosoever shall call upon the name of the Lord shall be saved. (Romans 10:13)

Talk to God today; repent of your sins; ask for His forgiveness; truly believe in your heart He will save you, that He is who He is; and trust in Him. Life is hard, and it's even harder without Christ in your corner. He never promised us an easy life or a life without pain, but He did promise that as His child, you will never have to face it alone. He will carry you through it.

GRIEF

Grief has a process, grief carries pain;
Grief is gonna change you, you'll never be the same.

Grief doesn't discriminate, doesn't care who you are;
Grief will always leave its mark, you'll bare the ugly scar

Grief will show who truly loves you,
But also brings those who will forever judge you

Grief tells you lies that you're dead inside
But Rest in God because that's where Joy abides

Grief has power to pull you down
But God is much stronger, He will turn your life around

When all hope seems lost and
there is nowhere to turn,
Lift up your eyes, Let God's love in you churn

He is the Giver of life, He gives and He takes
He is a Sovereign God, He makes no mistakes

He hears your cries and He knows your heart,
He promised to never leave or from us to part.

We can't see the picture and we don't understand
But God is the designer, He has a grander plan

Grief is hard and you'll want to give in
But Remember God's promise to hold your hand.

He will not leave you, He will mend your broken heart
Get in your Bible that's where it all starts!

He will pick you up and carry you through
As long as you let him, He'll give life that's new.

The scar will tarry, this will never change;
But in God's Grace, new love He will arrange

Grief will never leave you, it just eases with time
Just get up and move and let God's love shine.

IN GRIEF I FOUND YOU

In grief I found you, in my darkness you brought light
To feel you close I had to give up the fight

The devil he whispered your mine at last
Then Came God , Oh not so fast
You picked me up and held me tight
I surrendered to you with all of my might

I am so sorry for the life that I had chose
I had to lose everything
To Feel The God that I Now Know

I'm sorry I grieved you and pushed you so far
You had to break me, to leave a scar

I choose you God now and forever
My love for you is not up for surrender
You have my heart, mind and soul
Only you can fill the hole

I chose the world and it brought me pain
You saved me from myself and you changed the game

I give you my life for you I'll serve
Because your Grace has been more than I could ever deserve

Thank you Lord for not giving up on me
And breathing new life for others to see
To see Your Grace and your mercy shown
For a Chance in Heaven where none belong

Help me to be a witness to those in pain
By the lies Satan tells them there are no riches to gain

Help me to tell loves sweetest story
And how their Name can be written up in glory.

Trish Stanbery, a small-town country girl from Mocksville, North Carolina, unexpectedly found herself in a place she would have never imagined. She was a new wife who married her best friend. They bought their first house together in her hometown so she and her children could be close to family. She was living the life of her dreams until that fateful  day. It was a day that would rewrite her story.

That story is the one you will read in this book. It's a story of love and tragic loss, a story of family and forgiveness, a story beautifully penned in grief of how grace came in the mourning.

Printed in the USA
CPSIA information can be obtained
at www.ICGtesting.com
CBHW021316190724
11675CB00011B/143